The Charles

The Charles

The People's River

BY MAX HALL

DRG

DAVID R. GODINE *Publisher* Boston

First U.S. edition published in 1986 by
David R. Godine, Publisher, Inc.
Horticultural Hall, 300 Massachusetts Avenue
Boston, Massachusetts 02115

This book is an expansion and updating of "The People's River," an article in
Harvard Magazine, July-August 1984.

Library of Congress Cataloging in Publication Data
Hall, Max.
    The Charles, the people's river.
    "An expansion and updating of 'The people's river,'
an article in Harvard Magazine, July–August 1984"—T.p. verso.
    Includes index.
    1. Charles River (Mass.)—Description and travel—
Tours. 2. Charles River (Mass.)—History. 3. Charles
River Valley (Mass.)—Description and travel—Tours.
4. Charles River Valley (Mass.)—History. I. Title.
F72.C46H34   1986   974.4'4   85-45973
ISBN 0-87923-614-0

FIRST EDITION
Printed in the United States of America

To the memory of my father, Max R. Hall Sr.,
a real authority on rivers

Contents

List of Illustrations

Preface

The Charles first began to fascinate me in the summer of 1919, when I was nine years old. On my first trip outside Georgia, I spent four weeks visiting an aunt who lived near the present site of Boston University, in an apartment house facing the Charles River Basin. My diary says that I enjoyed the "Esplanard," took a two-mile motorboat trip for ten cents, and walked halfway across the "great Harvard bridge" that led to the "Boston Tech College." I doubt that I realized how new some of those things were at the time. The Massachusetts Institute of Technology had moved to Cambridge just three years before; ocean tides had been excluded from the Basin for only eleven years; and Boston's narrow Esplanade of that date was, like me, only nine years old. I made crayon drawings which were preserved by another aunt and which, on the suggestion of my publisher, David R. Godine, I am reproducing here for antiquarian rather than artistic reasons.

For a long time thereafter I had little experience of rivers, but I did have a river heritage. My father, Max R. Hall Sr. (1864–1939), a civil engineer, was the author or coauthor of ten or more books packed with descriptions and measurements of southern rivers. Beginning in 1902 he served the U.S. Geological Survey as its first District Hydrographer for the Southeastern States. In 1927, when he was Assistant Chief of Construction for the City of Atlanta,

The Charles River Basin in 1919, as seen by the author at age nine. The Gray & Davis factory in Cambridge, which made automobile starters, became the Jordan Marsh warehouse in 1929 and was demolished in 1974 to make way for the Hyatt Regency hotel.

A view downstream in 1919 from the vicinity of the present Boston University. Beyond the Harvard Bridge is Boston's "skyline," consisting of the State House dome and the Custom Tower.

the District Engineers of the Geological Survey expressed to him their "sincere appreciation of the pioneering work you did in developing the science of stream gaging."

My own curiosity about rivers leaped in 1943 when I traveled up and down the Tennessee River by boat, airplane, and automobile and wrote a series of ten articles about the Tennessee Valley Authority for the Associated Press.

When I moved to Cambridge in 1960, my ancient interest in the Charles started all over again. Increasingly, as the years passed, I wondered how the magnificent Basin got that way, where the river originated, what it was like upstream, and so on, and on, and on. In the 1970s, as a member of the editorial advisory committee of *Harvard Magazine*, I several times urged the editors to get somebody to write a good long article that would answer my questions. In the 1980s, as a contributing editor of that magazine, I undertook the job myself. The result occupied twenty pages of the magazine of July-August 1984. It was David Godine's idea that I should turn the magazine article into a book. Accordingly I have greatly expanded the text and almost tripled the number of illustrations.

In my study of the Charles, I received information and encouragement from many people.

I am especially grateful to Rita Barron, executive director of the Charles River Watershed Association. She provided me with the association's publications, put me in touch with specialists on various aspects of the Charles, and read and commented upon a draft of the magazine article. With her permission I have used a phrase of hers — "The People's River" — in the title of the article and of the book. An excellent writer, she has published much about the Charles and will publish much more, and I will remain one of her most appreciative readers.

I am also especially grateful to Christopher Reed, managing editor of *Harvard Magazine*, who listened to progress reports, gave me good advice, and commissioned drawings and photographs which enhanced the article and are being used again in the book. When I delivered an immensely long draft to the magazine, I assumed that it would have to be shortened for publication, but the editors gave me the supreme encouragement — they asked me not to cut but to lengthen it.

My heartfelt thanks go to the following people who contributed significantly to my learning process. On the evolution of the Boston Esplanade: Karl T. Haglund. On citizen participation in river improvements: Lydia Goodhue. On engineering: Arthur Doyle, K. P. Devenis, Edward C. Anders, Donald Harleman, and Edward P. Dunn. On fish, wildlife, and conservation: Joseph D. Bergin, Elissa Landre, Richard Cronin, Randall B. Fairbanks, Joseph D. DiCarlo, Phillips D. Brady, Theodore Chase, Stephen Bassett, and Lori Fafard. On pollution and sewers: Paul M. Hogan, Alfred F. Ferullo, Everett R. Kennedy, John Vetere, and Daniel K. O'Brien. On boating: D'Arcy MacMahon, Joseph Wolfson, Gail Pierson Cromwell, Harry Parker, Stephen E. Carr, David Thorndike, Buzz Tarlow, and Larry Smith. On anthropology: Dena F. Dincauze and Ives Goddard. On geology: Clifford A. Kaye. On industrial history: Michael Brewster Folsom, Alfred D. Chandler Jr., and Thelma Fleishman. On local history: Duscha Scott, Charles Sullivan, George M. Sanborn, Mary French, and Robert B. Hanson. On the source of the river: Robert T. Symonds. On Riverbend Park: Isabella Halsted.

Among those listed so far, Ed Anders and Al Ferullo are with the Metropolitan District Commission, and others at the MDC cooperated wonderfully, including Commissioner William J. Geary, Laura Palmer, Albert A. Swanson, Julia O'Brien, Paul DiPietro, James Falck, Charles Shurcliff, and Richard Feeney.

I also want to thank my daughters — Nancy for photography and Judy for editorial advice.

Of course I made use of published writings, including reports of official agencies. I found no books on the Charles published during the last forty years, but there was helpful information in many books that were mainly on other subjects — for example, *Boston: A Topographical History*, by Walter Muir Whitehill.

The Charles

1 Meet the Charles

The Boston Marathon starts in the town of Hopkinton, Massachusetts, and the contestants run 26 miles, 385 yards to the finish line in Boston's Back Bay. The Charles River, too, goes from Hopkinton to Boston, but it runs eighty miles.

This makes the Charles the longest river entirely within Massachusetts. Its brownish green water (sometimes blue under a blue sky) moves generally toward the northeast, but in the process flows repeatedly in every direction, both by small-scale meandering and by prodigious zig-zags from side to side of its drainage area.

The Charles, of course, is not famous for its size. Except for its last few miles, it is a rather small stream. In downtown Waltham, thirteen river miles from its mouth in Boston Harbor, it has an average flow of only 368 cubic feet per second, compared with 16,180 in the Connecticut River as it leaves Massachusetts and 7,474 in the Merrimack at Lowell. Even the modest Blackstone, a near neighbor of the Charles, averages 758 cubic feet per second as it crosses into Rhode Island.

Yet in some respects the Charles River stands out among the rivers of the world.

In its lower part it may be the best example anywhere of an urban river that has been radically reshaped and controlled in the

Overleaf: Cambridge and Boston and their mutual boundary, the curvaceous Charles, on May 21, 1984. View is approximately east-southeast. See map for names of the bridges, universities, and some other landmarks. (Photograph by Laurence Lowry for *Harvard Magazine*.)

service of the public. So far as I can discover, no other river passing through a densely populated coastal area has been transformed into a large fresh-water metropolitan lake whose level is lower than high tide in the harbor beyond. This lake, the Charles River Basin, is nine miles long. Its width is about 200 feet near its upper end in Watertown, about 400 feet at Harvard University (narrower at the Anderson Bridge), and about 2,000 feet in front of the Massachusetts Institute of Technology. The Basin provides the metropolitan area with a spectacular "water park," its green banks publicly owned and its surface spangled with boats.

Moreover, the entire eighty-mile river, rural, suburban, and urban, is increasingly protected and improved through the efforts of public agencies and private citizens. There are still many problems — the Charles was severely abused for a long time — but the trend has been unmistakably upward during the 1970s and 1980s. The City of Boston has been described by an architecture critic as a comparatively public city, where people for some reason feel they own the streets, parks, and waterfronts. This is even more true of the Charles. Rita Barron, executive director of a citizens' organization named the Charles River Watershed Association, who is the Charles's most militant defender and promoter, rightly calls it "the people's river."

There is no need to elaborate on the Charles as a passive scene of history and a symbol of intellectual accomplishment. Examples are well known. The country's first college — Harvard — was founded near the river; Paul Revere rowed across the Charles before he took to horse; General Washington commanded the new American army from a Cambridge mansion (now called the Longfellow House) with a fine view of the Charles; Old Ironsides was built at the river's mouth and is moored there now; the first telephone conversation o'erleaped the Charles; some of the earliest work on modern computers was done on an M.I.T. site that had been awash when the river was tidal.

Not so well known is the history of the Charles itself. The river has figured importantly in the development of American manufacturing, law, metropolitan government, civil engineering, and landscape architecture. The Charles has twenty dams, including a new one that cost $48 million and lengthened the fresh-water Basin by half a mile in the vicinity of Boston's North Station. Early bridges across the Charles were the country's largest at the time. The Charles has a man-made peculiarity more than three centuries old — at Dedham it loses part of its water to another river in a different watershed. The Charles provided Harvard with financial help for about two centuries. The Charles was the centerpiece of the nation's first venture into metropolitan government. The Charles is the scene of the world's biggest one-day rowing event. The Charles has what is believed to be the world's biggest public sailing program.

Map overleaf drawn by Charles C. Hefling Jr. for *Harvard Magazine.*

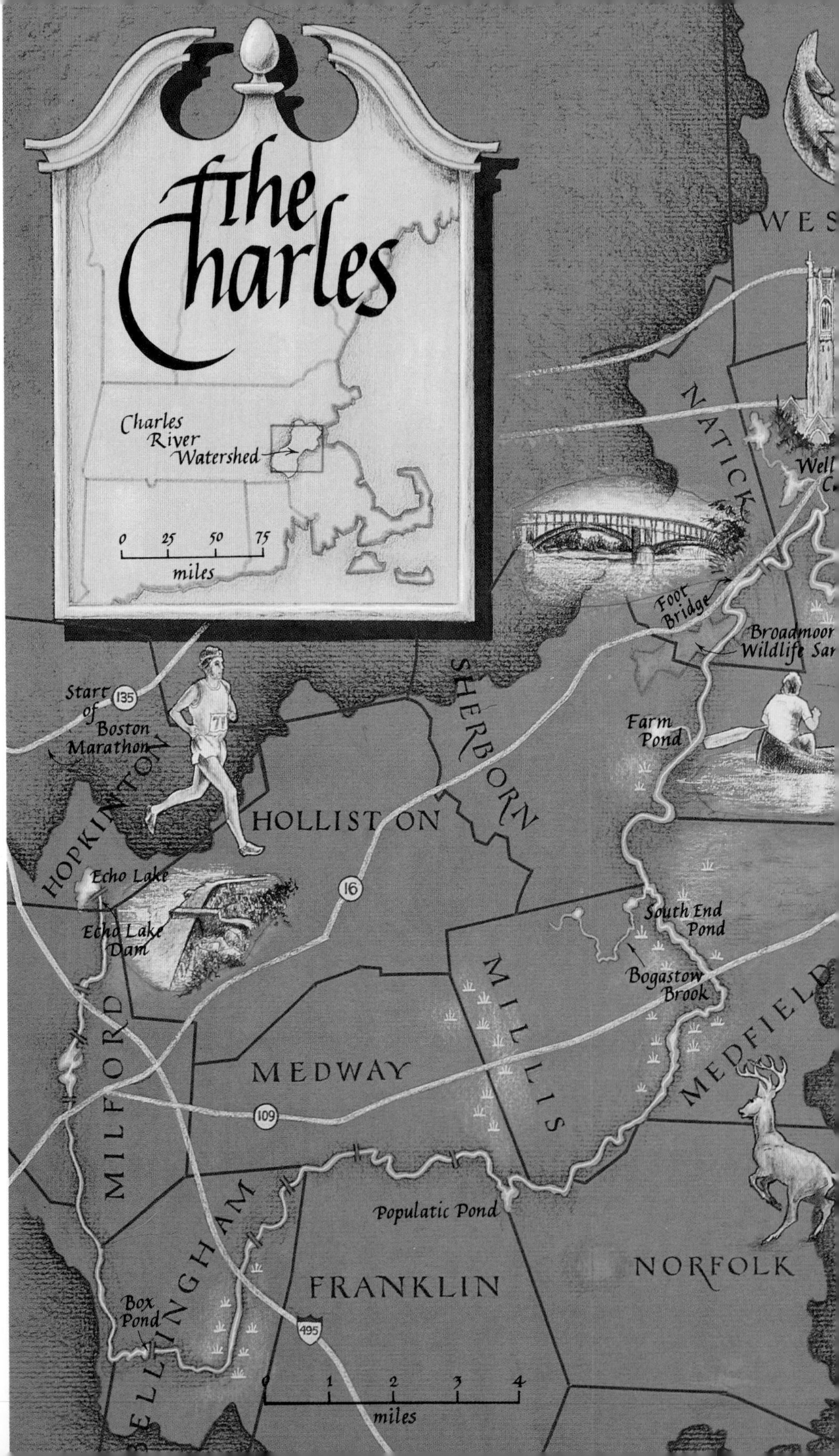

The Charles

Charles
River
Watershed

0   25   50   75
miles

WES

NATICK

Well
C...

Foot
Bridge

Broadmoor
Wildlife Sar...

Start of
Boston
Marathon

135

Farm
Pond

HOLLISTON

SHERBORN

HOPKINTON

Echo Lake

16

Echo Lake
Dam

South End
Pond

Bogastow
Brook

MILLIS

MILFORD

MEDWAY

MEDFIELD

109

Populatic Pond

NORFOLK

FRANKLIN

ELLINGHAM

Box
Pond

495

0   1   2   3   4
miles

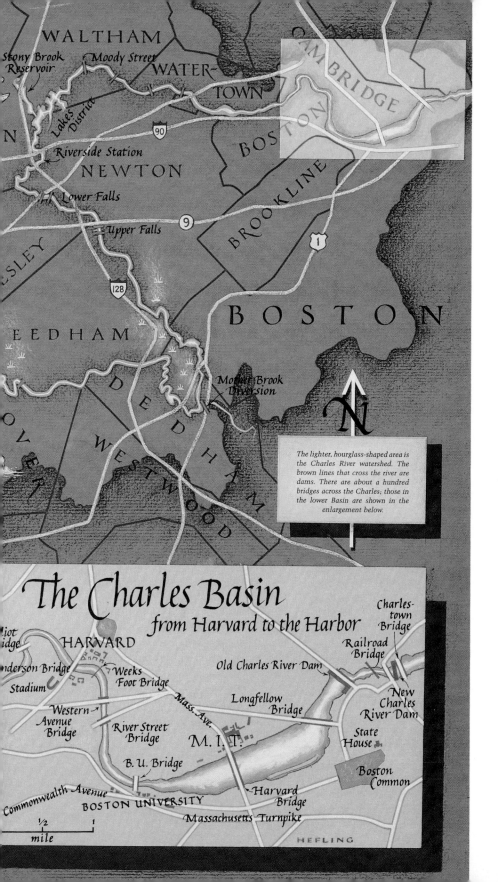

WALTHAM

Stony Brook
Reservoir

Moody Street

WATER-
TOWN

CAMBRIDGE

90

BOSTON

Lakes District

Riverside Station

NEWTON

Lower Falls

BROOKLINE

9

Upper Falls

1

128

ESLEY

EEDHAM

BOSTON

DEDHAM

WESTWOOD

OVA

Mother Brook
Diversion

N

The lighter, hourglass-shaped area is
the Charles River watershed. The
brown lines that cross the river are
dams. There are about a hundred
bridges across the Charles; those in
the lower Basin are shown in the
enlargement below.

The Charles Basin
from Harvard to the Harbor

Charles-
town
Bridge

iot
idge

HARVARD

Railroad
Bridge

nderson Bridge

Weeks
Foot Bridge

Old Charles River Dam

Stadium

New
Charles
River Dam

Western-
Avenue
Bridge

River Street
Bridge

Mass. Ave.

Longfellow
Bridge

M. I. T.

State
House

B. U. Bridge

Boston
Common

Commonwealth Avenue

BOSTON UNIVERSITY

Harvard
Bridge

Massachusetts Turnpike

½   1
mile

HEFLING

2 Down the Winding Stream

Naturally I had to see the source of the Charles. It was not like searching for the sources of the Nile. Even so, my river was more elusive than I expected.

The Charles begins in Echo Lake, which is mainly in Hopkinton. The lake is owned by the Milford Water Company, which retails water in Milford and wholesales it to Hopedale and Mendon. The company created the lake in two stages by building a twenty-two-foot-high granite dam across a miniature gorge in 1884

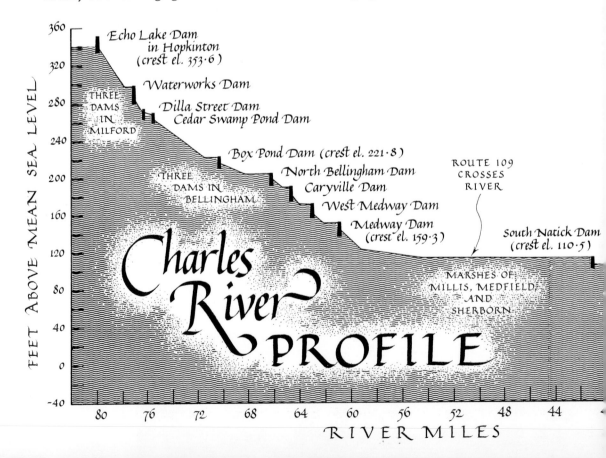

and adding ten feet in 1902. The lake is fed by several brooks, one of which springs from Honey Hill five hundred feet above sea level; but the Charles is officially considered to begin at the Echo Lake Dam, whose crest has an elevation of 353 feet, and that was my destination. The trek took place on an August day in 1983. I had the best of guides, Robert T. Symonds, who was then treasurer of the water company.

After scrambling and sliding (and falling down) along the rough lake shore, we reached the dam. It forms an arc, the ends pointing down river. Standing on the dam, I looked down river and was bewildered. There was no river, not even a trickle. Symonds explained that in the dry season, when the lake is not full, the Charles for its first mile or two consists of water flowing underground in a pipe twenty-four inches in diameter, bound for the waterworks in Milford to the south. In springtime, and indeed for about six months of the year, water spills over the dam and the river is visible, though it does not yet resemble a river.

That was a first lesson in the variability of the upper and middle Charles. Seasons and weather make a big difference. The flow at Waltham is many times as great in March as it is in September. And the variability comes also from the dams, creating ponds of different sizes and shapes. As the Army Corps of Engineers said in a 1972 report, it almost seems that "the Charles is more nearly a work of man than of nature."

After leaving Milford the stream continues southward, as if it

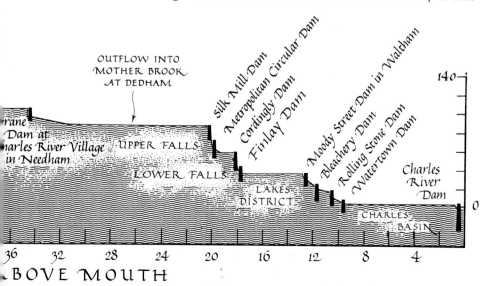

Drawn by Charles C. Hefling Jr. for *Harvard Magazine*.
SOURCE: U.S. ARMY CORPS OF ENGINEERS

were about to join the Blackstone and end up in Narragansett Bay. Just five miles from the Rhode Island border, it turns abruptly east, then north, then east again.

Past Medway, twenty river miles from Echo Lake and 220 feet lower, the stream enters a long stretch of gentle terrain, much of it marshy. Grassy marshes, swamps, and damp meadows make up more than ten percent of the 309 square miles of the Charles watershed. On a sunny October morning, paddling a canoe more or less northward with marshes of the town of Millis on my left and those of Medfield on my right, I guessed that the placid meandering river was about sixty feet wide. But in springtime it is many times that big. After a huge storm in March 1968, Arthur Doyle of the Army Corps of Engineers estimated the width at one mile, and he exclaimed to a colleague, "For Christ's sake, Jack, these things are acting just like our flood-control reservoirs!"

Next, the river carves northward through rocky hills (canoeists, beware of outcroppings from the river bed) and reaches its halfway point at South Natick, where the Puritan missionary John Eliot founded a settlement of his "praying Indians" in 1650. Less than two miles to the west is the rim of the Sudbury River watershed, which is a part of the Concord River watershed, which is a part of the Merrimack River watershed. But the Charles, just short of Wellesley College, makes a fantastic cloverleaf loop (see map) and flows approximately east for about twelve river miles, all the way to Dedham and the Boston section of West Roxbury, as if it were going to join the Neponset River and empty into Dorchester Bay at Quincy.

Indeed, part of the Charles does exactly that. It escapes through an outlet called Mother Brook. The place of egress is a strange sight. Streams connecting with rivers usually flow *into* them. Mother Brook, emerging from the river just across U.S. 1 from the Dedham Mall, pours out over a dam which the Metropolitan Dis-

Rambling river — the Charles in a typical pattern at Maple Swamp southwest of Medfield Center, fifty miles from its mouth. (Photograph by Laurence Lowry for *Harvard Magazine*.)

Mother Brook emerging from the Charles at Dedham. This photograph was taken in the rainy spring of 1984 when the water was high. Ordinarily more of the Mother Brook dam is visible. (Photograph by Edward C. Anders, Metropolitan District Commission.)

trict Commission raises and lowers to keep the Charles and the Neponset in balance. In accordance with an 1831 agreement the proportion of Charles water thus diverted is limited to one-third. The actual proportion varies widely. Typically it may be around twenty percent.

This extraordinary link between two river valleys originated in the need of Dedham's early inhabitants for bread. Grist mills and sawmills always follow pioneers. The story of the early mills and factories is well told by Thelma Fleishman in her booklet *Charles River Dams*, published by the Charles River Watershed Association. At Watertown, Thomas Mayhew had built a grist mill in

Silk Mill Dam as seen from Echo Bridge. The camera points south (upstream). Newton Upper Falls is at left, Needham at right. Mill buildings have been turned into a restaurant, offices, and shopping mall. The white water entering at left is the old spillway that ran under the silk mill. Echo Bridge carries an aqueduct (and pedestrians) across Hemlock Gorge. See the Charles River Profile (pages 10–11) for the locations of all dams on the river. (Photograph by Edward C. Anders, Metropolitan District Commission.)

1634. Dedham was founded in 1636 and immediately planned a mill on the river. But the river is slow-moving there, bordered by marshes, and a committee came up with a better idea — put the mill on Easte Brook, which rose about a hundred yards east of the Charles and ran fast eastward to the Neponset. All it needed was more water. They dug the connecting ditch in 1640. Later this was enlarged, and additional water wheels appeared along the stream. The name Mother Brook probably came into use before 1800. By that time the waterway was very controversial. Mill owners in the Neponset Valley depended on it. Farmers along the Charles liked the way it helped to drain their low-lying meadows. Mill owners down the Charles fought for a larger share of the water. Nowadays the diversion is used mainly for flood control.

At Dedham the Charles turns back on itself again and coils lazily inland, roughly parallel to Route 128, the circumferential highway. The river makes a big clockwise semicircle around the city of Newton, separating Newton from Needham, Wellesley, Weston, and, in places, Waltham and Watertown. At Upper Falls and Lower Falls it rushes over four dams between rocky bluffs, dropping fifty feet in about two miles. And shortly thereafter it begins to spread out into its "Lakes District," several miles long, having lily pads, coves, islands, good fishing, and good canoeing.

Near the upper end of the Lakes District, at the place where Route 128 tangles with the Massachusetts Turnpike (Route 90), there used to be two famous recreation areas, Norumbega and Riverside. Beginning in the 1890s, these spots attracted multitudes for canoeing and other activities. Both places flourished for decades and went out of style around the middle of this century.

Norumbega Park opened in 1897 on a hilly peninsula at the end of the Commonwealth Avenue Street Railway in Auburndale, which is a part of Newton. The park was developed by officials of the streetcar company, and it had a vaudeville theatre, restaurant, merry-go-round, bandstand, several boathouses, and a large zoo. Two steamboats made trips through the chain of lakes in summertime. In the big-band era of the forties and fifties a dance hall at Norumbega called the Totem Pole was immensely popular. The Totem Pole closed in 1964 and burned down in 1965. The site of Norumbega Park is now dominated by a Marriott hotel. But canoes are still for rent — at the Charles River Canoe Service near the spot where Route 30 (Commonwealth Avenue) crosses the river. And the Charles River Watershed Association has its headquarters there (2391 Commonwealth Avenue, Auburndale, Massachusetts 02166).

A northward view of Hemlock Gorge from Echo Bridge. The canoes are racing in the April 1984 "Run of the Charles" conducted by the Charles River Watershed Association. The two kayaks are competing in a special event. (Photograph by Jim Harrison for *Harvard Magazine*.)

Norumbega Park in Newton —
a bird's-eye drawing, about
1910. Commonwealth Avenue
is in the foreground. You are
looking approximately north
(downstream). The zoo and
theatre are at upper left. The
territory farther to the left,
beyond the river, is in the
town of Weston. (Jackson
Homestead Collection, Newton Historical Society.)

The Riverside Recreation Grounds opened in 1898 on forty acres in the town of Weston, just upstream from (that is, south of) Norumbega. The property had a half-acre swimming pool, tennis courts, a cinder track, football and baseball fields, and two big wooden buildings containing bedrooms, restaurant, dressing rooms, and boating facilities. There, one could rent not only an ordinary canoe or rowboat but a "war canoe" with seventeen paddles and room for ten passengers. A footbridge to the Newton shore connected the grounds to the Riverside depot of the Boston & Albany Railroad, near the present Riverside transit station. Thus, Bostonians could easily reach Riverside by train, just as they could reach Norumbega by streetcar.

The Riverside Recreation Grounds were built by a public-spirited Weston citizen, Charles W. Hubbard, at his own expense. He always expected to place them under public control, and in 1914 he gave the whole thing to the Metropolitan Park Commission. Meanwhile several boathouses had long since sprung up on the Newton side, and the whole Riverside–Norumbega area was crawling with pleasure craft. Even before the turn of the century it was estimated that 4,200 canoes were moored in the vicinity.

But the rise of the automobile, together with the rise of pollution in the Charles, eventually reduced the attractiveness of the Lakes District. The construction of Route 128 in 1949 chopped off part of the Riverside Recreation Grounds and damaged their beauty. The decrepit wooden buildings were destroyed by fire in 1959, just two months before they were to be demolished as unsafe.

The Lakes District came into existence in 1814 when a newly formed corporation called the Boston Manufacturing Company, led by Francis Cabot Lowell, Patrick Tracy Jackson, and Nathan Appleton, elevated an existing dam in Waltham, at the place where Moody Street now crosses the river. They used the resulting fall of water to produce cotton textiles on a scale never before known

Cordingly Dam at Lower Falls. A foot bridge above the rushing water connects Newton (*left*) with Wellesley. (Photograph by Edward C. Anders, Metropolitan District Commission.)

A scene at Riverside about 1900, in the era of canoe mania. Dusty scrapbooks in the office of Albert A. Swanson, the historian of the Metropolitan District Commission, tell of many accidents and some drownings in the Riverside-Norumbega area. In 1903 the metropolitan park police posted strict rules for canoeists. Among other things, couples were forbidden to recline side by side in a canoe. One couple was arrested for kissing. The Boston press gleefully reported their trial under large headlines. The man was fined $20; the woman didn't show up in court. (Jackson Homestead Collection, Newton Historical Society.)

in America. By that time Charles industry had gone beyond grist mills and sawmills. Iron products, paper, snuff, leather, and chocolate were being made at a number of locations, and small mills for spinning and other parts of the cloth-making process were increasing fast along the Charles and other New England rivers. But the mill of 1814 was something new, the first in the United States to use waterpowered looms and to integrate spinning and weaving in the same plant.

An earlier textile factory, the Slater Mill, had been founded in 1793 on the Blackstone River at Pawtucket, Rhode Island — the country's first power-operated spinning mill. The much larger Waltham establishment produced both thread and cloth, and was the first in America to manufacture cloth by means of powered machinery. It used so much water that it drew down the level of the Lakes District by several feet each day, creating mud flats which were covered again at night by the inflow of the river.

Alfred D. Chandler Jr., a historian at the Harvard Business School, attaches high importance to the Waltham mill. It led the same investors to expand in 1822 by founding the town of Lowell, Massachusetts, where the Merrimack afforded much more wheel-turning power. Waltham, however, continued to be an important

The Moody Street Dam at Waltham. This structure, thirteen feet high, is the highest dam on the Charles (not counting the Echo Lake Dam at the river's source). You are looking approximately north. The large building, which now contains housing for the elderly, used to be part of the Boston Manufacturing Company's cotton mill. Indeed the left-hand portion of it dates all the way back to 1814. In an adjoining structure is the Charles River Museum of Industry, presided over by Michael Brewster Folsom. (Photograph by Julia Giblin, Metropolitan District Commission.)

industrial town, both before and after steam reduced the importance of waterpower. Beginning in 1836 the big cotton mill at Waltham began using steam concurrently with waterpower, and continued to use both methods well into the twentieth century. About a mile upstream the Waltham Watch Company produced watches beside the river for about a hundred years until 1954 — but never with waterpower.

At Waltham the Charles heads east on the final leg of its journey to the Atlantic, having collected many small tributaries along its course. The tributary that drains the most territory is Bogastow

Brook, which enters the river in the town of Millis. Others bear such names as Hopping Brook, Mine Brook, Chicken Brook, Mill River, Sugar Brook, Stop River, and Waban Brook. (One of the many programs of the Charles River Watershed Association is called Adopt-A-Brook, in which schools and other organizations can lavish loving care on a little waterway.) In the north of the watershed is an important stream, Stony Brook, which forms the boundary between Weston and Waltham, but nearly all of it is impounded and piped into Cambridge's water supply. In the nine-mile Basin, below Watertown Dam, the only tributaries worth mentioning are the Muddy River and another Stony Brook, which enter the Charles through conduits near Fenway Park. Both discharge at times into the Back Bay Fens, a string of ponds and marshes which is a backwater of the Charles.

3   Before the English Arrived

The zig-zag Charles is a young river. For about a million years the whole area had been crunched intermittently by a series of glaciers coming and going, and the Charles in its present location probably developed around 11,000 years ago, when the most recent glacier was almost gone. The river's bizarre configuration was caused by several things, including glacial debris, the shape of the bedrock which the river encountered, and great hunks of slowly melting ice.

At that time the river extended farther east than it does now, because the ocean was about seventy feet lower then, according to Clifford Kaye of the U.S. Geological Survey. As the salt sea rose, it moved gradually up the river valley and enveloped what is now downtown Boston, leaving it very nearly an island topped by a ridge consisting of three high hills. What is now Boston's Back Bay was really a bay, a large cove of the Charles estuary. When sea level stabilized about 3,000 years ago, the river tides had reached their western limit, near the present location of Watertown Square. When the English shiploads began arriving in 1630, the river near the present Harvard Square wound *inland* twice a day and was bordered on both sides by broad salt marshes. And the site later to be occupied by M.I.T. contained oyster beds so large that they interfered with navigation.

The English, of course, were latecomers. Archaeologists have found evidence that human beings appeared in eastern Massachusetts almost as early as the Charles did. Little is known about them or their successors during the next ten or so millennia. It is possible that the Norse adventurer Leif Ericson passed along the coast about A.D. 1000, but the notion that Vikings actually settled on the Charles and left artifacts has no scientific support.

A century ago Eben N. Horsford, a chemist who developed processes for making condensed milk and baking powder, spent much time and money trying to prove the Viking presence. Norumbega, he believed, was an important Norse settlement and fort, and to commemorate its establishment he paid for an impressive stone tower in 1889. Norumbega Tower still stands in Weston, at the mouth of Stony Brook, across the Charles from the peninsula where Norumbega Park used to be. But Dena Dincauze, an anthropologist at the University of Massachusetts, Amherst, who directed an archaeological study of the Charles when she was at Harvard's Peabody Museum, says that Horsford's Viking artifacts are actually English artifacts of a later date. In 1968 she reported that the ditches and small banks which he believed to be Norse fortifications are similar to those in Millis and other towns, and probably were constructed as field boundaries and livestock fences in the seventeenth century.

The inhabitants encountered by the English were Massachusett Indians, speakers of a language of the Algonquian family. Apparently the only way they had changed the river was to build fish weirs — barriers of stakes, stones, and clay, causing fish to congregate and be more easily catchable.

In Newton a street named Quinobequin Road borders the Charles, and for about two centuries the statement has been appearing in print that the Indians called the river Quinobequin. The statement is not supported by historical evidence. As long ago as November 21, 1850, the *Cambridge Chronicle* published a letter from Thaddeus W. Harris, the Harvard librarian, in which he debunked the legend. His letter had little effect, but his argument was convincing. "Quinobequin" is more aptly applied to the Kennebec River in Maine. Apparently it became linked with the Charles through a misreading of old maps.

Not one of the early explorers seems to have reported that our river was called Quinobequin. Samuel Champlain, who investigated the coast in the years 1604 to 1607, passed a broad estuary that must have been the Charles and named it after a fellow explorer, Pierre du Guast — a name that fortunately did not stick. Champlain did not mention any Indian name for the Rivière du Guast. As for the Kennebec, he rendered it on his maps as "Quenibecque" and "Quinibequy," and the name went through many variations on Dutch maps during that century. John Ogilby's *America*, a well-known book published in London in 1670, contains a Dutch map in which the Kennebec is plainly labeled "Quinobequin." The same map shows the Charles in Massachusetts far to the southwest.

How then did "Quinobequin" get attached to the Charles? We now have to go back to 1614 when Captain John Smith came sailing along those shores. In his account of the voyage, the only Indian name he gave our river was the "Massachusets." Smith, like Champlain, drew a map of the region, but before publishing it he asked Prince Charles to change some of the Indian names to good British ones. The prince was fifteen years old, ten years short of becoming King Charles I. The map, as edited by the prince and published under the title "New England," showed that "Massachusets River" had been changed to "The River Charles." He also invented a "Boston" and a "Cambridge," long before the real Boston and Cambridge were founded in America. He placed them not on the Charles but in what is now Maine. Cambridge was his new name for an Indian town which Smith rendered "Aumuckcawgen" and also "Anmoughcawgen." This town was on a river which Smith called the "Sagadahock," and which Prince Charles renamed the "Forth," and which was none other than the Kennebec.

In 1797 the *American Gazetteer*, compiled by Jedidiah Morse, said the Charles was "called anciently Quinobequin," and this was repeated in other gazetteers and histories and became generally accepted as a fact. It seems likely that Morse, or some person on whom he relied, had seen Cambridge on John Smith's map, situated on a river which the authoritative Dutch mapmakers had called Quinobequin — and had jumped to a wrong conclusion.

One more note on Indian names: Ives Goddard, an anthropologist at the Smithsonian Institution, thinks it likely that the Massachusett Indian term *Mushauwomuk*, which the English shortened to *Shawmut* and which literally means "where there is a big river," referred not just to the Boston peninsula but to the estuary and its adjacent lands.

4 Ferries and Bridges

After the English had planted settlements at sundry spots along the Charles, sooner or later there were bound to be disputes about the use of the water.

In the eighteenth and nineteenth centuries there was a fundamental change in the legal concept of property in America. The static common-law principle that an owner was entitled to undisturbed enjoyment of his property gave way gradually to a dynamic view that emphasized productive use, economic development, and the needs of the community. So says Morton J. Horwitz of the Harvard Law School in his prize-winning book *The Transformation of American Law, 1780–1860*. He argues that the greatest impact on this trend came from the evolving law of water rights, and that the most dramatic departure from common-law principles took place in Massachusetts.

The Charles participated in this transformation of law in several ways:

• Its industrial development and its pond-interrupted shape were promoted by the eighteenth-century mill acts of Massachusetts, which was far ahead of other states in conferring privileges on proprietors of mills (be they grist, cotton, or other) in order to promote economic growth. Owners whose property was damaged by a dam were supposed to be compensated, but the damage could be done without prior court approval.

• Some of the court decisions that contributed to the doctrinal trends arose from the Charles. In general, property owners fighting the mill proprietors got less and less satisfaction, especially in the 1820s, when the textile industry really surged.

• The lower Charles was the battleground of the great Charles River Bridge case, settled by the Jacksonian Supreme Court in 1837. Legal historians consider this case a mighty victory for rapid technological advance over privileged property forms. Harvard and its faculty members were deeply involved. For one thing, the university was receiving part of the toll revenues from the bridge. Moreover, the two men who were ably running the Law School at the time, Simon Greenleaf and Joseph Story, were major figures in the case — on opposite sides of the issue.

Harvard's involvement will become clearer when we look at the early history of toll ferries and toll bridges on the tidewater Charles.

The first and most important ferry, begun in 1631, linked the Boston peninsula with the Charlestown peninsula, and it afforded the shortest route to Cambridge and points west. (See map on next page showing Boston and Cambridge in the seventeenth century.) In 1640, just after Henry Dunster became Harvard's first president, at a time when the destitute little college was struggling to exist, the Massachusetts authorities awarded this ferry privilege to Harvard. The college leased out the facilities and collected rent on them until 1785. The amount seems to have been £30 a year at first, Harvard's only regular income from outside sources, and it gradually increased.

True, this Charlestown ferry income dipped a little when the "Great Bridge" was completed between Cambridge and Brighton in 1662, replacing a ferry there. This was the first bridge across the Charles east of Watertown and was said to be the first of considerable size in the colonies. A low wooden drawbridge that always seemed to need repairing or rebuilding, it crossed about where the Anderson Bridge now stands. At the Cambridge approach a causeway was erected over the marsh — a southward extension of Wood Street, later Brighton Street, still later Boylston Street, and now John F. Kennedy Street.

But the southern route from Harvard to the center of Boston via the Great Bridge and Roxbury was eight miles, almost twice as long as the way through Charlestown. The real threat to the ferry privilege would be the construction of a bridge down river, and eventually this dire event came to pass. In 1785, soon after Harvard had spent £300 to repair the four-boat Charlestown ferry and was beginning to receive rent of £200 a year, a corporation consisting of John Hancock and eighty-three others obtained a state charter to build the Charles River Bridge at the site of the ferry. They opened it in 1786 on the eleventh anniversary of the Battle of Bunker Hill with much firing of cannon and an estimated 20,000 spectators. The bridge was 1,503 feet long (about 1,100 between abutments). It achieved fame as the greatest American bridge, indeed the first to be thrown across a broad river. Harvard's ferry achieved instant death. Harvard, however, claimed that its grant was a perpetual privilege, and its claim was honored to the extent that the bridge corporation was required to compensate the college by annual payments of £200 ($666.66 in the new American currency) during the time when the bridge was to remain a commercial venture (forty years, extended to seventy).

The Charles River Bridge was such a financial success that in 1793 it was followed by the West Boston Bridge, even longer than the first, linking Boston with Cambridge on the site of the present Longfellow Bridge. The West Boston Bridge had important eco-

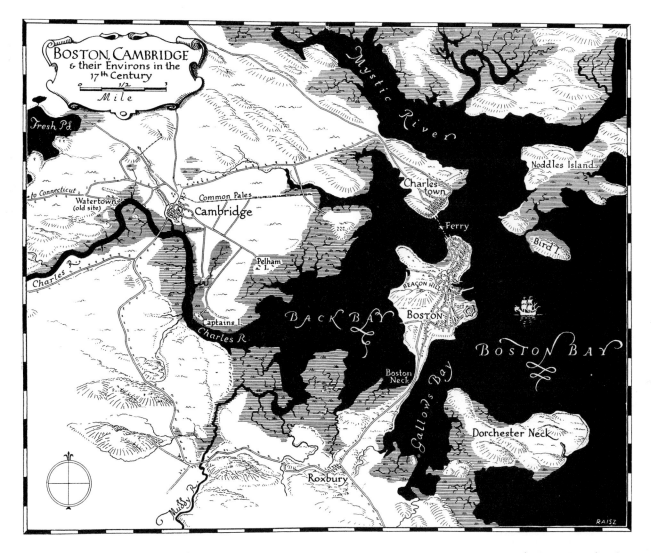

Drawn by Erwin Raisz for *The Founding of Harvard College* by Samuel Eliot Morison (Harvard University Press, 1935).

nomic effects on both Boston and Cambridge. In 1809 a third toll bridge, known as Craigie's Bridge and also as Canal Bridge, brought Boston and East Cambridge together. Then came two other bridges where the estuary was narrower — at River Street (1810) and Western Avenue (1824). All these bridges contained draws to permit masted vessels to sail up and down the Charles. Indeed, the estuary had nothing but drawbridges until the construction of the present Longfellow Bridge with its towers resembling salt and pepper shakers. That impressive structure, which now bears the Cambridge subway tracks, was completed in 1906 and was at first called simply Cambridge Bridge.

The historic legal battle mentioned earlier began in 1828 when the state authorized a second Charlestown toll bridge, the Warren Bridge, right next door to the Charles River Bridge. The new bridge was completed that same year. The owners of the Charles River Bridge, claiming an exclusive privilege, tried unsuccessfully to

The tidewater Charles in 1775, as depicted in a model at Harvard's Widener Library. View is east-southeast, as in the modern aerial photograph shown earlier. *Lower left*: Harvard Yard. *Lower right*: A masted ship, faintly visible at the mouth of Town Creek. In the background (*left of center*) is Boston with its three high hills, looking like one hill from this angle. The wide part of the river to the right of the hills is the Back Bay, not yet filled in. (Photograph by Christopher S. Johnson for *Harvard Magazine*.)

prevent the construction and continued to press their claim for nine years until the Supreme Court ruled against them.

Chief among the victorious lawyers for the Warren Bridge was Simon Greenleaf. Joseph Story, who served on the Supreme Court the whole time he was at the Law School, feared for the sanctity of property rights and made a vigorous dissent to Chief Justice Roger Taney's majority opinion. Stanley I. Kutler, writing a book about the case, said Greenleaf's leave of absence from Harvard was a milestone in the history of academic freedom, because the university had a stake in a victory for the old bridge, not only receiving compensatory tolls but also owning shares in the bridge corporation. Nevertheless Harvard's old ferry privilege was still so respected that the Warren Bridge was required by the state to share in the compensatory payments. Thus Harvard got money from both bridges, and to some extent from the state, until the bridges became toll-free in the 1850s. There is a disagreement on the extent of Harvard's revenue. One estimate, by Professor Seymour Harris, was that the total received between 1786 and 1856 was around $60,000.

5   Transforming the Basin

Meanwhile the irregular Charles estuary was shrinking — not only figuratively, by bridges, but also literally, by fills. The estuary was so broad that the early explorers overestimated the size of the inland river. Today the Charles River Basin is flanked by more than two square miles of reclaimed land — some of the most expensive real estate in the world.

Walter Muir Whitehill, in his *Boston: A Topographical History*, tells how Bostonians expanded their city by lowering its three hills sixty feet or so and throwing the dirt into the water.

Beginning in 1799 they moved the top of Mount Vernon, the westernmost rise, into the Back Bay around Charles Street. Between 1810 and 1824 they used the top of Beacon Hill to obliterate a large salt pond in the North End, south of Causeway Street. In 1835 the top of Pemberton Hill was torn off to extend the North End beyond Causeway Street.

A little earlier, around 1820, a mill dam bearing a toll road a mile and a half long had been pushed across the Back Bay where Beacon Street now runs. The tides rushing through mill sluices were supposed to operate a complex of factories, but the main effect of the mill dam was to create what Whitehill called "an unsightly and stinking nuisance." Between 1857 and about 1880 the Commonwealth, the city, and various private proprietors performed the mammoth feat of filling in the Back Bay and creating a new section bounded as follows: on the north by Beacon Street and the

Boston's tidal Back Bay from the State House dome in 1858. Beacon Street, then a mill dam, is shown stretching westward into the distance. The water to its left became solid ground during the next twenty years. At left of picture are Boston Common and the Public Garden. The shoreline was then at Arlington Street. (Boston Athenaeum.)

reduced Charles, on the east by the Public Garden, on the south by railroad tracks, and on the west by the Fens, which were all that remained of the bay, and which the city acquired for a park in 1877. This time the fill came from Needham, not far from the river at Upper Falls. It was glacial gravel scooped out with a wondrous machine called the steam shovel (recently invented in Philadelphia) and hauled to Boston on railroad trains shuttling day and night.

All this and other rearrangements made Boston a new city, but twice a day the old Charles still rose and fell nearly ten vertical feet, and at low tide a lot of the river bottom was exposed, and not just along the banks. The smell was hideous, and conditions grew worse as the river became fouler with the pollution from industry

Low tide at Mount Auburn Street in Cambridge around 1887. View is eastward toward Harvard Square. On the wharf is a stone yard, where stone brought by schooner is being cut for construction purposes. (Harvard University Archives.)

and fast-multiplying households. Tidal currents were swift and dangerous.

In the eighties and nineties there was increasing realization that something had to be done. The municipalities systematically took title to most of the shores of the wide salt river. Seawalls were built on both sides, and dredges scraped the river bottom and pumped mud over the walls to create new territory, especially in Cambridge where the marshes extended far inland.

The process in Cambridge was speeded by the initiative of Charles Davenport, who had manufactured carriages and railroad cars near the waterfront. He bought up large amounts of cheap wetlands and, with others, formed the Charles River Embankment Company in 1881. This company won the right to develop its property for a luxurious residential section like Boston's Back Bay, with the understanding that it would convey to the City of Cambridge a river-front esplanade two hundred feet wide and a strip of land for an approach to a new bridge that was being planned.

Left: Low tide in the Lower Basin around the turn of the century. View is upstream; the new Cambridge seawall is at right. (M.I.T. Museum.)

Right: Hydraulic dredge filling Cambridge wetlands in 1898. View is eastward (downstream), with Boston at right. Mud from the river bottom is being pumped over the seawall. Dredges with long shoots like this were first used to dig the Suez Canal in the 1860s. (M.I.T. Museum.)

The residential section never materialized, mainly because a railroad that had been built across the marshes attracted fine factories rather than fine homes. But the esplanade with its carriage drive came into being, and so did the bridge. The Harvard Bridge (named after John Harvard) was opened in 1891. It entered Boston via a street named West Chester Park. It entered Cambridge via a long causeway over the wetlands where M.I.T. would transplant itself in 1916. Both West Chester Park and the causeway are now called Massachusetts Avenue.

By this time a historic movement had begun for further measures that would turn the river liability into an asset on the order of the world-famous water park on the Alster River in Hamburg, Germany, eighty miles from the North Sea.

In the years just before and after the turn of the century, many public officials and private citizens took part in the crusade for a river that would contribute more to the health, recreation, aesthetic pleasure, and economic attractiveness of the metropolitan region. It is probably fair to choose four men for special mention:

Harvard Bridge soon after its
1891 completion. Boston is in
the background. That part of
Massachusetts Avenue in foreground was then only a causeway over the Cambridge wetlands. The Massachusetts
Institute of Technology was
later built on filled land to left
of causeway between the river
and the railroad. (M.I.T.
Museum.)

Harvard Bridge from its Boston
end around 1923. On the Cambridge side is the monumental
new M.I.T. building, completed in 1916. To the left is Riverbank Court, an apartment
house built in 1900, about the
time when the Cambridge
Esplanade (now Memorial
Drive) was opened. (M.I.T.
Museum.)

Four who were active in making a metropolitan park system with the Charles Basin at its heart: Eliot the landscape architect, Higginson and Storrow the civic leaders, Freeman the civil engineer. (Freeman picture from M.I.T. Museum, others from Harvard University Archives.)

Charles Eliot

Henry Lee Higginson

James J. Storrow

John R. Freeman

• Charles Eliot (1859–1897), landscape architect.

• Henry Lee Higginson (1834–1919), the very prototype of the wealthy public-spirited Bostonian.

•James Jackson Storrow (1864–1926), who, like Higginson before him, was called "Boston's first citizen."

• John Ripley Freeman (1855–1932), civil engineer.

Although Charles Eliot lived but thirty-seven years, his name stands high in the profession of landscape architecture, and the general public ought to be better acquainted with him. A son of Harvard president Charles William Eliot, he joined the firm of Frederick Law Olmsted in 1883 soon after graduating from the university. By 1890 young Eliot was publicly urging lovers of nature to "rally to preserve for themselves and all the people" the scenes of beauty that still existed near their doors, just as Boston's lovers of art had united to establish the Museum of Fine Arts. In 1891 he founded the Trustees of Reservations, a nonprofit organization which now owns (or has obtained conservation restrictions on) more than 125 properties in Massachusetts, preserving them for environmental purposes. More than twenty-five of the land parcels — well over 2,500 acres — are in the Charles Valley.

In 1892 the Trustees of Reservations brought together the park officials of Boston and its neighboring cities and towns, with the result that Massachusetts created the Metropolitan Park Commission that same year. Eliot was its landscape architect and is considered the father of that agency. A Metropolitan Sewerage Commission had been established in 1889 (reputed to be the oldest metropolitan service district in the country); a Metropolitan Water Commission was established in 1895; and in 1900 those two commissions merged.

In 1919 they were united with the park commission to form the

Metropolitan District Commission (MDC), which eventually came to serve 2,500,000 people in fifty-four communities in one or more ways — parks, water, sewerage. Among its many duties the MDC has jurisdiction over the lower half of the Charles — the forty-mile stretch from the South Natick Dam to the mouth. In 1985 the sewerage function of the MDC was put into a new agency, the Massachusetts Water Resources Authority.

Charles Eliot's vision of the Charles River was influential and prophetic. For example, he wrote in 1894 that "a bridge will be required in the bend of the river at Gerry's Landing" and a parkway thence to Fresh Pond. When they finally built this bridge in 1951 they named it the Eliot Bridge after both President Eliot and his son. At the dedication ceremony Charles was fittingly described as "one of the first conspicuous advocates of ignoring municipal boundaries in matters that plainly transcend them."

The principal key to the dreamed-of water park was a dam across the river to keep out the tides. In 1894 the Metropolitan Park Commission and the State Board of Health made a joint study and recommended the dam. But the State Board of Harbor and Land Commissioners held hearings and reported in 1895 that the dam might damage the harbor. At that time there was a widespread belief, later proved wrong, that the harbor was kept from filling up by the "scouring" effect of the ebbing waters of rivers and creeks.

The most determined enemies of the dam were property owners on the water side of Beacon Street, whose back windows overlooked the river. They argued that a fresh-water basin might cause malaria and other bad things; but the part of the dam proposal that they disliked most was a plan to fill a strip of the Basin three hundred feet wide and pay for the dam by selling the new land for a row of residences appropriate to a water park, between Beacon Street and the river. The Beacon Streeters forced abandonment of

Backsides of Beacon Street houses in 1901 when the Charles was still tidal. The photographer stood on Harvard Bridge looking east toward downtown Boston. (Courtesy of Shurcliff & Merrill, landscape architects.)

that plan, and for years it seemed that they had defeated the dam itself.

In 1901 the proposal for a dam was revived under the leadership of Henry Higginson and James Storrow, fellow members of a Boston banking firm. Supporting them were Charles William Eliot, Augustus Hemenway, John F. Fitzgerald, and other prominent figures.

Higginson's prestige and money were important to the cause. He had joined the family firm of Lee, Higginson in 1868 after serving as an officer in the Civil War. In 1881 he had founded the Boston Symphony Orchestra, and he was still financing it. In 1890 he had donated Soldiers Field to Harvard University, which he had attended as a freshman.

Storrow's exertions for the dam were even more important. He was the most active organizer of the movement. Storrow was thirty years younger than Higginson. In 1885 he had captained a

Harvard crew that beat Yale by seventy-five seconds (a quarter of a mile). He had risen fast in the legal profession and then had joined Lee, Higginson in 1900. Storrow was obsessed with the idea of making the Charles a place of beauty, recreation, and health for all Boston residents of whatever status.

The Storrow-Higginson group published pamphlets, sent out a circular letter, received several thousand favorable replies, and persuaded the Massachusetts legislature to create another investigating body: the Committee on Charles River Dam. Its chairman was Henry Smith Pritchett, the M.I.T. president. Storrow and Higginson engaged as legal counsel Nathan Matthews, former Boston mayor, who had eloquently called for a dam in his inaugural address of 1891. Storrow himself was the opening witness at the committee's hearings. By now the proposal to sell residential lots between Beacon Street and the river had been dropped.

John R. Freeman was appointed chief engineer of the committee. Thanks to him more than to anyone else, the study was monumentally thorough and the final report in 1903 was irresistible. Freeman was an M.I.T. graduate and an active member of the M.I.T. Corporation. In 1981 the American Society of Civil Engineers paid tribute to him when it designated the Charles Basin as a "National Historic Civil Engineering Landmark." To celebrate the occasion, the Boston section of the society published a special edition of its Journal in the summer of 1981 containing an essay on how the dam was won, along with several other documents, including Freeman's brilliant report. Since 1978 the Basin has also been on the National Register of Historic Places.

The legislature accepted the advice of the committee in 1903, and the dam was built on the site of Craigie bridge, which connected Boston with Lechmere Point in East Cambridge. The work was carried out by a new triumvirate, the Charles River Basin Commission, headed by Henry Pritchett — the same influential man who had chaired the Committee on Charles River Dam. The chief engineer was Hiram A. Miller, and the consulting engineer was Frederic P. Stearns. A lock for navigation, 350 feet long and forty-five feet wide, was built at the Boston end. Near the Cambridge end were nine sluices — channels which could be opened or closed as necessary. The middle sluice was also a lock for very small boats.

Tides were excluded from the Basin on October 20, 1908, when about eighty wooden gates in a temporary "shut-off dam" were simultaneously dropped into place while dignitaries congratulated one another and boat whistles tooted and screeched. Men quickly began piling mud and gravel against the timber wall. Thereupon the locks and sluices went into operation.

Thus the Charles River Basin came into existence in 1908. Work continued on the permanent dam. It consisted of earth bounded by masonry walls and was wide enough for a spacious park and a highway, which were finished in 1910. The highway crossed the large lock via a drawbridge. From 1907 to 1912 the Boston Elevated Railway Company built an arched concrete viaduct across the river, almost flush with the downstream wall of the dam, in order to carry streetcars to Lechmere. The park on the dam was eventually obliterated by the Museum of Science, which took over an existing structure in 1951 and steadily expanded.

Although the water below the dam continued to rise and fall, the new Basin was kept almost stable, about seven feet above mean low tide and about two feet below mean high tide. Boston Harbor has a mean tidal swing of 9.5 feet, which is very large for the United States. The Basin could not be set above high tide without flooding some of the filled-in parts of Boston and Cambridge. The present Storrow Drive, for example, is lower than the average high tide and about 3.5 feet lower than high tide in a typical storm.

The Charles flowed through the 1908 dam via the sluices, except that twice a day, when the tide came up, these channels were

Old Charles River Dam and its park. Date of picture is unknown, but it was certainly taken before the Museum of Science began occupying the park in the 1950s. East Cambridge with its Lechmere Canal is in foreground; downtown Boston and its harbor are beyond. The large lock is at the Boston end. The arched viaduct, carrying streetcars between Boston and Lechmere, parallels the downstream edge of the dam. (Metropolitan District Commission.)

Old Charles River Dam in 1976. The Museum of Science has filled up the park. Boston buildings have filled part of the sky. (Photograph by Jack Maley, Metropolitan District Commission.)

closed to prevent a reverse flow. During the seventy years when that dam was in operation the Basin never entirely freed itself of salt. Though fresh water continuously flowed into the upper end, it did not sweep all the salinity before it, for salt water is heavier than fresh water and much of it sat on the bottom. Moreover the sea kept infiltrating through the big lock and leaks in the sluices. Indeed, there was a great infusion of brine on the very day of the shut-off in 1908, because a long drought had reduced the river's flow so much that filling the Basin with fresh water would have taken an unacceptable length of time. The Basin Commission reported in 1909 that this had been the only "disappointing feature" of the birth of the Basin as it assumed its constant level.

During the battle over the dam, some of its opponents claimed that the whole scheme was an attempt to provide the boating men of Harvard with a better place to row. Even today the idea persists that boat racing was an important motive for damming the river.

No doubt boating was one factor. For example, the following statement appears in the 1901 report to the Harvard Overseers by their "Committee on Physical Training, Athletic Sports and Sanitary Conditions of All Buildings," whose chairman was George W. Weld of Weld Boathouse distinction: "The question of the proposed dam across the Charles River was also duly considered and all the members pledged themselves to do everything in their power to carry out our plans for it."

But to suggest that Harvard rowing was the main motive for building the dam would be very far off the mark. Counsel for the Higginson group told the investigating committee in 1902 that several hundred letters had been written to dispose of the "frivolous suggestion" that only the rowing interests of Harvard University would be benefited by the proposed basin, for there were 500,000 persons in the Charles Valley whose health and recreation would be enhanced when what was "little more than a mudhole" was replaced by "the most extensive, most central and most beautiful parks to be found in any great city in the world."

The dam, however, was not all that was needed. Before people could truly use and enjoy the water park, the harsh, vertical, uninteresting, and almost inaccessible Boston edge of the Basin had to be turned into parkland. This job started before the dam was built and continued for decades thereafter. The work was done in four stages, about twenty years apart.

The first stage, around 1890, was the Charlesbank in Boston's West End, just upstream from the site where the dam was to be. The Charlesbank was a pioneer playground designed by Frederick

The Boston Embankment after 1910. It became popularly known as "the Esplanade." View is west (upstream) toward Harvard Bridge. Side by side with the new strip of land is Back Street. Some forty years later, Storrow Drive was built on this embankment. At bottom of picture is Embankment Road. (Courtesy of Shurcliff & Merrill, landscape architects.)

Law Olmsted for the residents of that crowded district. The firm of Olmsted, Olmsted & Eliot also produced plans for a system of parks and parkways extending far up both sides of the river.

The second stage was the making of the "Boston Embankment" at the time the dam was built. From 1906 to 1910 Pritchett's Basin Commission laid a new seawall and dredged up a new strip of land that started at the Charlesbank and reached upstream a mile and a half to Charlesgate West, where Olmsted's Fenway Park met the Charles. The lower segment of the strip was wide enough to include a street, which they named Embankment Road. To the distress of the commission, the rest of the strip could not accommodate both a park and a road, because the legislature had restricted its width to one hundred feet. This part of the embankment went side by side with Back Street, a small private way that hitherto had been the only thing between the seawall and the Beacon Streeters' drab back yards and stables. Work on the Boston Embankment was at first delayed because the Boston Transit Commission planned a subway beneath it but never was able to set a construction date. The finished embankment with its grass and walkways was popularly called "the Esplanade," and Bostonians were proud of it.

The third and fourth stages of development came in the early thirties and early fifties. The principal designer in each case was Arthur A. Shurcliff (1870–1957), who was also the landscape architect for Colonial Williamsburg. He had studied under Charles Eliot and worked for Olmsted, Olmsted & Eliot before going on his own. In 1905 he conceived the idea of a majestic island in the Basin. The notion was taken up by others and seriously considered from time to time for more than twenty years before sinking like Atlantis.

The third stage of Boston riverbank development began in 1928 with the appointment of a Special Commission on the Charles

River Basin, headed by Henry I. Harriman. During the next few years the authorities greatly widened and lengthened the embankment. They made a lagoon, a sheltered boat landing, space for concerts, and other improvements. Shurcliff designed irregular sloping banks instead of a straight seawall, and this change was the salvation of water sports. Ironically, the lower Basin had not proved to be a good place for racing shells and other small boats because the perpendicular Boston wall had rebounded the waves and thereby had accentuated the roughness of windswept water. The Harriman Commission also recommended more bathing beaches like Magazine Beach, which was still in use on the Cambridge side just upstream of the Cottage Farm Bridge (now Boston University Bridge), but the increasing pollution of the Basin thwarted that proposal.

Part of the cost of the Basin improvements was covered by a million-dollar gift from Helen Osborne Storrow, the widow of James J. Storrow. The Esplanade was renamed the Storrow Memorial Embankment. An able chronicler of these events, Karl T. Haglund, in an unpublished paper called "The Charles River Basin and the Politics of Park Design" (1985), says it was this embankment that finally created the glorious water park in the image of

Springtime on Boston's Esplanade. Three scenes on or near the lagoons. (Photographs by Jack Maley, Metropolitan District Commission.)

DOCTOR PAUL DUDLEY WHITE BICYCLE PATH

Left: The Esplanade on the Fourth of July in 1977. The time is 6:30 P.M. and crowds are gathering for the evening concert and fireworks. Storrow Drive is at right. (Photograph by Jack Maley, Metropolitan District Commission.)

Right: The Fourth of July in 1985. View is westward toward Harvard Bridge. The Hatch Shell is at lower center, Storrow Drive at left. Already at 5:00 P.M. there are multitudes on the Esplanade and in boats. In midstream are the barges from which the fireworks will be launched. (Photograph by Jack Maley, Metropolitan District Commission.)

58   THE CHARLES

Very early morning at the boat landing. Sailboat masts stand in a row. This picture was taken from Longfellow Bridge. The old John Hancock Building casts its shadow on the new one. (Photograph by Bill Hartmann.)

Hamburg or Venice "about which Bostonians had fantasized for sixty years."

By now the automobile was fast changing the metropolitan area, and one of the main recommendations of the Harriman Commission in 1928 was that a highway be placed on the widened embankment in order to reduce traffic in the Back Bay and fill a missing link in the Basin's parkway system. This proposal caused a fierce controversy and was dropped in 1929. But the proposal emerged more strongly in the 1940s, and after another intense battle it was approved by the legislature in 1949.

Thus the fourth stage of riverbank development, in the early fifties, included Storrow Drive — named after James J. Storrow. It was built parallel to Back Street on the filled land that was the original Boston Embankment of 1910, and the Back Bay was again cut off from the river. But at least the Esplanade was not reduced in size. Through the efforts of the chief opponents of the drive — the Storrow Memorial Embankment Protective Association led by Donald Starr — the legislature authorized another widening to compensate for the territory lost to the highway. Shurcliff proceeded to design the present enlarged system of lagoons, narrow islands, and little pedestrian bridges that is shown in the accompanying photographs.

6 A University and a River

When the constant-level Basin was created in 1908, Harvard University had already turned its face southward toward the river after about two centuries of looking the other way.

In those early centuries the Charles had served mainly as Harvard's commercial link with the sea. For example, from about 1800 to 1827 the college sloop *Harvard* had brought firewood from Maine to the college wharf on Town Creek where the north end of Kirkland House is now. Students sometimes swam in the swift tidal river, and more than one drowned.

The Cambridge riverfront near Harvard changed in the 1850s when a dike was laid along the shore and most of the marshland was drained; and by 1877 all of Town Creek had been filled in. But the dry land thus created did not belong to Harvard and became covered with residences and with commercial establishments including car barns, coal docks, and a power station.

Even so, the Charles was steadily assuming a larger place in student life. The impetus for this was the growth of organized sports.

The earliest one was boating. Samuel Eliot Morison wrote that "Harvard discovered the Charles" when a boat club was formed in 1844 and raced two Boston crews on the still-liquid Back Bay. Other boat clubs materialized. The first Harvard-Yale race took place on

Lake Winnepesaukee in 1852 (it has twice taken place on the Charles, in 1946 and 1974). Crimson was first used as the Harvard color at a Boston City Regatta in 1858. The University Boathouse was built in 1869 near the present Dunster House and served until 1900.

Intercollegiate baseball at Harvard began in the 1860s. Intercollegiate football began in the 1870s. So did intercollegiate track meets. These sports were played on Cambridge fields where the Law School and Harkness Commons now stand; but in time it was recognized that their manifest destiny was across the river on the spacious flatlands of Brighton, a town which was annexed by Boston in 1874.

The old Boylston Street drawbridge at Harvard University before it was replaced by the Anderson Bridge. The Harvard Stadium, in background, had been built in 1903. (From 1912 annual report of Metropolitan Park Commission, courtesy of Metropolitan District Commission.)

The brand-new Anderson Bridge in 1913. (From 1913 annual report of Metropolitan Park Commission, courtesy of Metropolitan District Commission.)

The way was prepared through philanthropy. Henry Wadsworth Longfellow, hearing that slaughterhouses might be built on the Brighton Meadows in plain view of his Brattle Street home, bought seventy acres there as a gift for Harvard. He persuaded thirteen friends and relatives to join him in the donation, which took place in 1870. Twenty years later Henry Higginson made his famous gift of Soldiers Field, a thirty-one-acre tract, in memory of six of his Civil War friends. (He first called it "The Soldier's Field," and later "The Soldiers' Field," but for a long time now the official version has done without the "the" and the apostrophe.) At the time of his gift in 1890 the university bought a strip along the shore, supplementing the Longfellow and Higginson parcels.

Navy on the Charles. View is upstream from Anderson Bridge in 1918. In that year much of Harvard was occupied by the U.S. Naval Radio School. The white boathouse on the Cambridge shore at upper right, near the foot of Ash Street, is the Cambridge Boat Club, built in 1909. In 1947 it was bodily moved upstream to its present location at Gerry's Landing, where it is visible in the next picture. (Harvard University Archives.)

Marshes were drained as more space was needed, and in the late nineties, two sports buildings were planted on that side of the river. One was Carey Cage, with its facilities for indoor baseball practice. The other was Newell Boathouse, which was and is the home of Harvard's varsity oarsmen. It promptly burned down and as promptly sprang up again in 1900. Most impressive of all, in 1903 the colossal Harvard Stadium reared itself on Soldiers Field and became the capital of American football.

Harvard was a national football power in those years, and the new stadium gave Harvard and Boston a chronic case of football fever. On football Saturdays some spectators came by water, and others approached through Brighton, but most of them had to

Eliot Bridge under construction in 1950 (*near center of picture*). The finished structure may be seen in the lower portion of the large aerial picture near beginning of book. View here is approximately northeast. On the Boston side, at upper right, is Soldiers Field Road curving around Harvard playing fields. Along the Cambridge shore, at left, is a brand-new stretch of Memorial Drive, passing Mount Auburn Hospital. At lower center is Buckingham Browne & Nichols school. (Cambridge Historical Commission.)

negotiate a bottleneck, the ramshackle wooden bridge of 1862 at Boylston Street, a descendant of the Great Bridge of 1662. The *Harvard Lampoon* took note of the congestion by a parody of Longfellow's "The Bridge." Concerning the West Boston Bridge (whose successor was to be named for him), Longfellow wrote:

> I stood on the bridge at midnight,
> As the clocks were striking the hour,
> And the moon rose o'er the city
> Behind the dark church tower.

The Lampoon said of the old stadium bridge:

> I stood on the bridge at midnight,
> I had left the field at five.

By 1908, when the dam increased the attractiveness of the Charles, the need for a new stadium bridge was glaring. Larz Anderson '88, United States ambassador to Belgium, met the need. He gave the Metropolitan Park Commission the funds for a handsome bridge, 440 feet long including approaches, as a memorial to his father, Nicholas Longworth Anderson '58. The Anderson Bridge, often informally called the Larz Anderson Bridge, was completed in 1913. It was made of brick and concrete to harmonize with the fence around Soldiers Field and with the Weld Boathouse of 1907 on the Cambridge side.

Throughout this century Harvard has been consolidating its position athwart the Charles. On the Cambridge side the university acquired most of the former marshland along the river east of Boylston Street. Again philanthropy made it possible: Edward W. Forbes and some of his friends had systematically bought the properties in order to give them to Harvard. The university completed three freshman dormitories there in 1916 and another in 1926, and incorporated these dormitories into the new upperclass House system starting in 1930. Industrial buildings on both sides of the river vanished. The new home of the Harvard Business School arose on the south bank in 1926 and 1927. The John W. Weeks Bridge for pedestrians bent gracefully over the river at the same time. The athletic facilities near the Stadium expanded. In the 1970s a subway yard and shop, dating from 1912, gave way to the Kennedy School of Government and the MDC-owned John F. Kennedy Park between the school and the river. As a result of all this, the Charles as it curves through Harvard, especially the stretch between the Anderson and Weeks bridges, is an artistic masterpiece — perhaps one of mankind's more successful attempts to bring architecture and nature together in a harmonious relationship.

7 Flood Control

The Charles River Basin, for all its natural and man-made beauty, was vulnerable in a way not foreseen by its makers. Unwelcome guests visited Massachusetts in 1954 and 1955: Carol and Diane, two of New England's worst hurricanes. Diane hurled twelve inches of rain onto the Boston area in two days of August 1955. The dam of 1908 had not been designed primarily for flood control (neither had the old dams up the river) and anyhow conditions had changed. The downpour, along with the instant runoff from the greatly expanded asphalt jungles of the metropolitan area, caused the Basin to rise four and a half feet above normal and to back up through drainage systems into streets and basements. Damage was estimated at $5.5 million, which would be several times that much at today's prices. Harvard alone suffered damage estimated at between $60,000 and $100,000. The water could not flow out through the dam fast enough — and not at all when the tide was higher than the Basin.

What should be done? The hurricanes, especially Diane, brought the Charles under close scrutiny again, as in the time of John R. Freeman half a century before. Two engineering firms made a series of studies for the Metropolitan District Commission and recommended a pumping station to hasten the departure of water from the Basin when necessary.

There was no room for this station on the existing dam, but after much testing a suitable place for a new dam was found half a mile closer to Boston Harbor, where the Warren Bridge of 1828 had been. One of the firms, CE Maguire Inc., completed a design for the dam in 1964. Peter Devenis was in charge of the design work, and it was he who originated the idea of the pumping station.

The same company designed the Amelia Earhart Dam for the MDC on the short Mystic River, not far north of the mouth of the Charles. That dam, completed in 1966, excluded the tides but had no pumping station (pumps were added later). The new Charles River Dam with its pumps would be much more expensive, and the MDC could not get the money for it. No new hurricanes had hit Massachusetts, and the plan for a new dam became controversial. So the idea grew that the Army Corps of Engineers ought to investigate the whole flood-control problem in the valley of the Charles.

This was a time of increasing public concern over the environment, and the sorry condition of the Charles had begun to alarm more of the people who lived near it. In 1963 the Leagues of Women Voters in cities and towns along the river formed a Charles River Valley Group to study the waterway and reach a consensus for action. Lydia Goodhue, president of the Wellesley League, took the initiative in organizing the Valley Group and later became its chairman. Very little information was then available about the Charles; the new group dug up its own information and vigorously circulated it. The Charles River Watershed Association was founded in 1965 and gradually increased its influence under the leadership of Kenneth H. Wood.

The Corps of Engineers in Washington, under the authority of Congress, had told its regional offices that a federal interest existed in "comprehensive planning" of water resources and that watershed studies could be initiated by the public works committees of Congress. In June 1965 the House Committee on Public Works called for a comprehensive survey of the Charles River watershed, and the New England Division of the Corps of Engineers was ordered to make a five-year study.

From the beginning, the Corps sought and welcomed wide participation. It held three public hearings in January 1967, was guided throughout by a Coordinating Committee of federal and state agencies, and asked President Nathan Pusey of Harvard to organize a Citizen Advisory Committee. This committee, of which Thomas D. Cabot was chairman, was more active than the Corps expected. Its members not only received reports and commented on them but also attended meetings of the Coordinating Committee and spoke up freely. They also publicized the Corps' proposals and helped get them approved in Washington. The Corps in its final report acknowledged the committee's assistance as the "ombudsman for the watershed residents." And it acknowledged valuable help from four nongovernmental bodies: the Charles River Watershed Association; the Valley Group of the League of Women Voters; the Massachusetts Audubon Society; and the Trustees of Reservations.

The Corps in 1968 and 1972 came up with a two-part program of flood control, one part *structural*, the other *nonstructural*.

In the structural part, the Corps confirmed the need for the new Charles River Dam, which would have a pumping station and three locks. Congress approved this in 1968. Construction began in 1974 and was finished just in time for the blizzard of February 7, 1978, which caused a monstrous tide of fifteen feet above mean low water (five and a half feet above mean high water). This equaled the highest Boston tide on record, that of April 16, 1851. The engineers blocked out the sea by temporarily closing the locks and sluices, and they ran all the new pumps to keep the

snow-fed river from overflowing its banks. The Army Engineers turned the new dam over to the MDC, but that agency could not begin regular operations until 1981 when it completed a treatment and pumping plant at Prison Point in Charlestown to keep sewage out of the half-mile extension of the Basin.

At that time the original Charles River Dam stopped being a dam; its big lock and its sluices are permanently open. (But the old drawbridge still delays traffic when sizable boats go through the open lock.)

According to a financial officer of the Corps of Engineers, the new Charles River Dam — including the design and construction of the pumping station, locks, pedestrian walkway, fish passages, and other installations at the immediate site — cost $48 million

(85 percent of it from the Army and 15 from the MDC). The higher figures that are often quoted — from $60 million up to $76 million — include the cost of the Prison Point treatment station, the conduits necessary for its operation, and various other parts of the whole Charles Basin project.

The pumping station is one of the mightiest in the United States. It has six propeller-type pumps with total capacity of 8,400 cubic feet per second, which is greater than the average flow of the Merrimack at Lowell. Edward C. Anders, MDC resident engineer, put it this way: more than four million gallons a minute. The pumps are driven by six diesel engines, each of 2,700 horsepower. These enormous engines roar into action when precipitation or melting snow along the Charles threatens to raise the Basin to an undesirable level. The pumps pull water straight up from the bottom of the Basin into chambers from which it rushes down chutes into the tidal river on the other side of the dam.

In the spring of 1984 the pumps operated more than usual. March was snowy and rainy, and rain fell again in April. From one to four pumps were in action from time to time between March 29 and April 13, keeping the Basin steady. During the week of Monday, May 28, something like a monsoon flooded New England. In a six-day period Boston had 7.2 inches of rain, 4.12 inches on May 31 alone. But the Charles got off fairly lightly. Rainfall was more intense in the Connecticut Valley and other areas. More important for the urban Charles Basin, the big pumps in the dam, running no more than four at a time, took the storm in stride. Storrow Drive had some flooding, but not from the river. Without the pumps, Storrow and much else would have been under water.

Though flood control was the main reason for the new Charles River Dam, the structure also met other needs. It speeded navigation by having three locks — two of them two hundred feet long for pleasure boats and another one, three hundred feet long, for

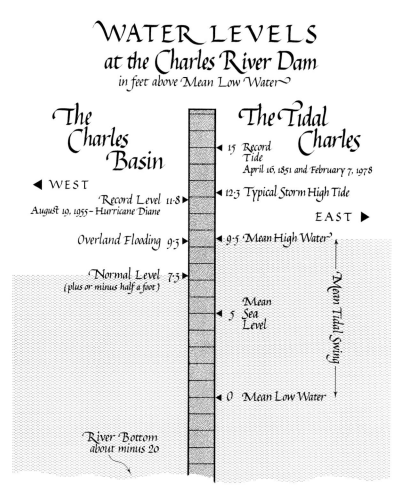

WATER LEVELS
at the Charles River Dam
in feet above Mean Low Water

Compiled by the author; drawn by Charles C. Hefling Jr. for *Harvard Magazine*.

The Charles Basin

The Tidal Charles

◄ WEST

◄ 15 Record Tide
April 16, 1851 and February 7, 1978

Record Level 11·8 ►

◄ 12·3 Typical Storm High Tide

EAST ►

August 19, 1955 – Hurricane Diane

Overland Flooding 9·3 ►

◄ 9·5 Mean High Water

Normal Level 7·3 ►
(plus or minus half a foot)

Mean Tidal Swing

◄ 5 Mean Sea Level

◄ 0 Mean Low Water

River Bottom about minus 20

the few commercial vessels that still poke into the Basin. Some summer days all three locks are used. On July 4, 1985, they handled 1,621 boat passages, a new one-day record, and the use of the locks has been growing each year. (The locks were named after Colonel Richard Gridley, the first head of the Army Engineers, who supervised the fortifications for the Battle of Bunker Hill in 1775.) The dam also reduced the salinity of the Charles, for its locks and sluices were designed to inhibit the upstream passage of salt water from the harbor and to encourage the downstream passage of salt water from the depths of the Basin. At the Boston end of the dam is a station for MDC police boats. At the Charlestown end is a tiny new park named after Paul Revere.

The dam with its red-brick pumping station has won several awards. In January 1985 it was one of thirteen winners (out of 630 entries) of the newly established Presidential Award for Design Excellence. The jury was headed by I. M. Pei. The honor was shared by CE Maguire Inc. and the New England Division of the Army Corps of Engineers.

The nonstructural part of the five-year Charles River Study is entitled Natural Valley Storage (NVS). The Corps of Engineers calls it the first and only nonstructural flood control project in the United States. Instead of building dams to create storage reservoirs, the Corps set out to prevent future floods by ensuring that the *natural* reservoirs, the wetlands of the Charles Valley, would not be developed into fast-runoff places like Boston and Cambridge. The Corps proposed this innovative scheme in 1972; Congress approved it in 1974; and it was completed in September 1983 at a cost of $8.5 million.

Natural Valley Storage grew out of the following circumstances. Nearly all of the rising of the Basin in heavy storms is caused by urban and suburban runoff, not by water flowing down from the upper and middle river. Flood crests up around Millis and Medfield take four or five days to reach Boston, and by that time the Basin can accommodate them. Their slow passage is caused by the wetlands. The river simply spreads out into low-lying undeveloped areas, which then gradually discharge their waters back into the mainstream. The engineers were impressed by this phenomenon during the deluge of March 1968. They calculated that if forty percent of the wetlands were drained for commercial and residential development the control of floods would require dams and dikes costing perhaps $100 million. Better to preserve the wetlands.

To this purpose the New England Division of the Corps of Engineers purchased outright 3,252 acres in 439 tracts along the upper two thirds of the Charles and its tributaries. The state's Division of Fisheries and Wildlife is managing most of those tracts, under lease from the Corps. The Corps also obtained easements on several thousand more acres, which did not change ownership but must be left in their natural state.

Natural Valley Storage was not invented by any one person; the concept evolved as the study went on. Conservationists had long favored restrictions on the use of wetlands, but they were not thinking primarily of flood control, nor did they offer the benefit-to-cost ratios that were required of the Corps. The Corps had no general authority to "buy wetlands," but it could "buy reservoir lands." Some time passed before the two concepts merged. Arthur Doyle, a civilian who became project director of the study in 1970, at first favored a modest plan of acquiring and strengthening a dozen roadways to act as control dams. He gives much credit to Elliot Childs, chief hydrologist of the New England Corps, for assembling the scientific data that permitted an expansion of the scheme. Doyle and others were struck by the future run-off dangers in case of commercial development along the new Route 495 and elsewhere.

When the Corps recommended Natural Valley Storage in 1972, the idea was so novel in Washington that its approval was in doubt. Massachusetts citizens pressed for action. Senator Edward Kennedy took up their cause. He spoke at a crucial Senate hearing on May 2, 1973, and further strong testimony was given by representatives of citizens' groups.

Flood-control measures are often blamed for disturbing the balance of nature, but in this case flood control and conservation are working together.

8 The Cleanup

At the same time, the notorious pollution of the Charles has been under vigorous attack, again with the help of federal funds. Efforts to clean up the river go back a long time. In the nineteenth century the industrialized Charles became a horror. In 1892 Boston's Engineering Department listed 416 sources of pollution, from Milford to Boston. Among them were the industrial and human wastes of factories, the blood and floor-washings of the Brighton abattoir, and the raw sewage of nearly the whole population of Cambridge.

Heroic measures and new conditions have wrought big changes since then. The first step was the construction of two metropolitan trunk sewers by the Metropolitan Sewerage Commission just before and after the turn of the century. These trunk lines intercepted sewage from the areas north and south of the river and bore it to islands for discharge into Boston Harbor. Treatment plants were later built on the islands.

Over the decades, industrial pollution dwindled for various reasons — including changes in the kinds of industry — and is no longer such a serious problem on the Charles. Nevertheless, the metropolitan and municipal sewers could not stay ahead of the region's population growth. Even as late as 1970 the river as a whole may not have been more sanitary than in 1900.

Then more federal money became available — anywhere from fifty to ninety percent of the cost of major projects, typically seventy-five percent. Paul M. Hogan of the state's Division of

Water Pollution Control estimates that from the late sixties to 1985 a total of about $2 billion was spent in Massachusetts for pollution abatement, and that at least $100 million of it was spent in the Charles River Watershed.

The upper Charles was much improved by regional "advanced treatment" plants in Medway and Medfield, and in 1985 another was nearing completion in Milford. At the same time the construction of new conduits is enlarging the scope of the advanced facilities. For example, the "secondary" treatment plant at Millis, which was discharging into Sugar Brook and thence into the Charles, has been connected to the superior treatment plant in Medway. The Charles above Watertown is rated Class B (swimmable-fishable), and most of the time, except in a few spots, it probably lives up to its rating.

So far the river is not exactly teeming with swimmers, for it lacks good beaches and public confidence. One drawback is the olive-green murkiness. This could inhibit rescues of swimmers who get in trouble, and it bothers the authorities. The color, however, is not a sign of health dangers; it comes mainly from vegetation in the wetlands, releasing color as a tea bag does. Clear water is not a characteristic of streams in eastern Massachusetts. The Charles River Watershed Association conducts annual swims in the swimmable part of the Charles. Rita Barron says, "We cannot continue to reject a healthy natural system just on the basis of color." During one of these annual swims — on a hot Saturday in July 1985 at Novitiate Park in Newton — I found that the river felt good and smelled good. Standing in knee-high water near the bank, I could not see my feet, but this did not make the swimming unpleasant.

The nine-mile Charles River Basin is definitely *not* rated swimmable. In the summer of 1984 the official counts of bacteria were many times the standard for a Class B rating.

Swimmers in the Charles. The scene is Novitiate Park, Newton, in July 1985 when the Charles River Watershed Association conducted its annual swim. The other shore, 150 feet away, is in Needham. The City of Newton acquired Novitiate Park in 1980 with the aid of state funds as a result of a citizens' movement led by a non-profit, volunteer organization called the Newton Conservators. (Photograph by Linda Mackey, Newton Conservators.)

One frustrating problem in the Basin, only partly solved, is that of "combined sewers." Sewer pipes under the streets of Boston, Cambridge, and many other communities were designed to carry both street runoff and sewage to the big metropolitan sewers. The trouble was that the system could not accommodate all of this combined flow during a heavy rain. Overflow points had to be provided, else water would back up and flood the cities. At these overflow points, polluted water escaped into the river. A good deal of it still does. Even in dry weather there are some direct flows of polluted water into the Basin, but the overflows during storms are much worse.

One line of attack on the problem has been to replace the combined pipes with two separate systems. This is what has been going on in Cambridge, for example. In the autumn of 1983 the city's "Phase V" was finished — the construction of separate systems in the area west of Massachusetts Avenue and south of Upland Road. By then about two-thirds of the Cambridge sewers had been separated. Then the project was interrupted for lack of funds. City officials hope that the two remaining phases — in north and west Cambridge — can be finished around 1990.

But the replacement of *Boston's* combined sewers would be a crushing task, costing perhaps $3 billion. Therefore another approach was devised. In 1971 the MDC opened a plant called the Cottage Farm Detention and Chlorination Facility, on the Cambridge side just upstream of the Boston University Bridge. This station, designed by CE Maguire Inc., is connected to some of Boston's overflow points by a conduit under the river and is connected to Cambridge overflow points via the North Charles Relief Sewer, which the MDC built along the Cambridge riverbank in the late sixties and early seventies in order to help the historic, overburdened North Charles Sewer in its task of bearing sewage to Boston Harbor. In a storm, much of the overflow from both sides of the river is collected here for screening, settling, chlorination, and storage in huge tanks; and when the tanks are full, the excess is released to the river. After the storm, what is left, including solid matter, proceeds in the normal way to the treatment plant on Deer Island.

The opening of the Cottage Farm station probably marked a turning point in the campaign to clean up the Basin, in the opinion of Alfred F. Ferullo, director of Environmental Quality in the MDC Watershed Management Division. The Prison Point plant of 1981, mentioned earlier, treats polluted storm overflows in the same way the Cottage Farm station does, and pumps the chlorinated wastewater to a point below the new Charles River Dam. But Ferullo is far from saying that these facilities are enough to bring about a satisfactory bacteria count. The truth seems to be that several costly plants are needed, particularly on the Boston side. An upgrading of the Cottage Farm station would help.

The combined-sewer problem is especially acute in the Back Bay Fens, where the volume of wastewater is far too great to be handled by the Cottage Farm station. Nothing much can be done about this without huge funding, which may not soon be available. The famous Fens, owned by the City of Boston, are the single worst source of pollution in the Charles Basin.

Another longstanding pollution problem in the Basin seems all but conquered. This was the problem of salt water on the river bottom, a stagnant layer that was not conducive to healthy aquatic life. The Basin is typically ten to fifteen feet deep at Harvard, and the lower Basin is typically about twenty feet with some holes that exceed thirty-five. When organic matter settled to the salt layer it used up the dissolved oxygen there and, in decomposing, generated hydrogen sulfide. So the Basin sometimes smelled like rotten eggs. (There are still some odors near culverts where sewage enters, especially at the Cottage Farm station after heavy rains, but hydrogen sulfide is no longer the culprit.)

The salinity problem was handled in two ways. The new Charles River Dam was designed so as to reduce the infiltration, as already mentioned. Also, the MDC installed six diffusers, or "bubblers," on the river bottom to "destratify" the water — that is, mix the fresh and the briny so that all would be aerated and would move out to the harbor together.

Each bubbler consists of a length of perforated pipe through which compressed air is forced. A considerable boiling is visible on the surface. A champion sculler, Gail Pierson Cromwell, told me that a bubbler once rocked her boat — a scary experience.

The bubblers, installed in 1978 and 1979, did their job well. The MDC says that the bottom salinity, which used to measure about seventeen pounds of salt per 1,000 pounds of water, was reduced to two pounds or less. The state's Division of Water Pollution Control in 1984 found "virtually no salt" in the Basin from Watertown to a point downstream of the Longfellow Bridge. The six bubblers are still in position, but in the mid-eighties only two of them were considered necessary.

The Basin may never be a good place to swim. Even if all sewage is some day diverted, there will still be runoff from the streets of some of the densest urban areas in existence. Certainly in the 1980s the Basin is not fit for swimmers. And that raises the question whether it poses a health threat to boaters who capsize. Joseph Wolfson, president of Community Boating, Inc., which conducts a large sailing program in the Basin, told me in the fall of 1985: "We have three or four hundred capsizes a year, and I've never known anyone to get sick." Others point out that there is no reliable body of scientific evidence on the question. The problem — if it is a problem — has become more visible with the rise of boardsailing, also called windsurfing. People who engage in that sport capsize a lot more frequently than conventional sailors.

What about "acid rain"? Recent studies seem to show that the main stem of the Charles stands up to it very well. Some of the tributaries give more indications of acidity, either from acid rain or natural sources. Rivers in general, and particularly urban rivers with their alkaline inflows such as sewage (treated or untreated) and urban runoff, resist acidity better than ponds and lakes in remote areas.

The Massachusetts Water Resources Authority, mentioned earlier, was approved by the legislature in December 1984 and came into existence July 1, 1985. It assumed responsibility for all of the MDC's sewerage division and part of its water-supply function. The MDC continued its jurisdiction over the metropolitan rivers and their adjoining parks and parkways. The MDC, in fact, operates many thousands of acres of parklands along with roads, beaches, pools, rinks, bridges, dams, other flood-control projects, and the third largest police force in New England. It also controls the Quabbin and other reservoirs, as well as the watershed lands surrounding them.

The formation of the Massachusetts Water Resources Authority was a result of pollution — not in the Charles but in Boston Harbor. The treatment station on Deer Island was in wretched condition, and a harbor cleanup was obviously going to take many years and cost billions of dollars. In the MDC's view, the state's tax-limitation law of 1980 known as "Proposition 2½" ruled out such financing and even prevented proper maintenance of the existing facilities. At any rate the pollution worsened, the City of Quincy sued the MDC, and the legislature boiled with proposals for action. The upshot was that the governor, the MDC commissioner, a Superior Court judge, and key legislators all agreed that only an independent authority with power to issue revenue bonds could raise the money for a full cleanup. The new authority was not subject to Propositon 2½ or to certain pay and personnel regulations that apply to state agencies.

Some people, including John W. Sears, who had been the MDC commissioner from 1970 to 1975, felt that the cause of metropolitan government had been set back for decades. MDC Commissioner William J. Geary, a park enthusiast who had taken office in February 1983, did not think so.

Geary told me in an interview in the summer of 1985, "Our agency is stronger now because this has focused our mission. We are primarily a parks agency, a preserver and reclaimer of open space in the tradition of Olmsted and Eliot. That proud heritage is not diminished in 1985. It is more urgent than ever. A park is a *common meeting ground*, for rich and poor, for everybody. That fascinates me."

9 Fish and Wildlife

The marshy Charles, its water quality improving and its wetlands increasingly protected, entertains an abundance of fish and other fauna. It is a "wildlife corridor," the connector of the long line of open spaces preserved by the Trustees of Reservations, Army Engineers, Audubon Society, town and city governments, and citizens who maintain large parcels of unspoiled land on the river.

Elissa Landre, who directs the Broadmoor Wildlife Sanctuary of the Massachusetts Audubon Society, a tract of 577 acres along the Charles in Natick and Sherborn, speaks with enthusiasm of the creatures that roam, swim, or fly this corridor. Here is a brief sampling: white-tailed deer, red foxes, river otters, minks, muskrats, snapping turtles up to thirty pounds or so, great blue herons, great horned owls, ospreys, and red-tailed hawks. The Charles wetlands are a major habitat of waterfowl. Some stay the year but most are passing through in spring or fall — though not necessarily in a hurry to leave. The wood duck and mallard and some other migratory species use the area for breeding. The little red-white-and-green wood ducks nest in hollow trees (or boxes placed in trees), sometimes a mile or two from the mainstream. The young wood ducks emerge from the nest-hole one day after hatching, make a daredevil plunge to the ground, and immediately head for water. Among the multitude of songbirds visiting the valley are brightly colored wood warblers, gluttons for Charles River mosquitoes. And Elissa Landre, with a light in her eye, may even show you one of her special interests — blue-spotted salamanders, very rare in Massachusetts.

As for fish, the Charles contains at least twenty-nine species and is much more popular as a fishery than a swimmery.

The river's midsection, between Medway and Watertown, is "well known, verging on famous" for large-mouth bass up to five pounds or so, according to Joseph D. Bergin, an aquatic biologist for the state, and also has chain pickerel up to two feet long. Bergin said he would have no qualms about eating fish from those waters. In the Lakes District the carp and sunfish became so plentiful that fierce tiger muskies and northern pike were imported to control their populations. The carp weigh as much as twenty-four pounds (occasionally perhaps more) and are the biggest fish in the Charles. On a spring Sunday the banks upstream of the South Natick Dam are apt to be lined with people reducing their grocery bills by catching panfish such as bluegills and pumpkinseed. Into the far upper Charles several thousand trout from hatcheries are dumped every April and are caught within about two weeks.

The broad lower Basin, too, contains plenty of life — catfish, goldfish, killifish, mummichog, and others — but various obstacles including public distrust inhibit fishing, a circumstance disappointing to Richard Cronin, director of the state's Division of Fisheries and Wildlife. He led me to a window of his aerie in the Saltonstall Building, pointed down to the magnificent Basin, and said, "Right out there is a sleeping giant, an untapped resource. Look at that! Twenty or thirty sailboats, and not a single fishing boat." Not everyone shares Cronin's enthusiasm.

For an observer who is not an avid angler, the most interesting fish in the Charles are those called *catadromous*, meaning that

Fishing near Watertown Square, just downstream of the Galen Street Bridge. This spot near the extreme upper end of the Charles River Basin was tidal until 1908. (Photograph by Jack Maley, Metropolitan District Commission.)

they are residents of fresh water but go to sea in order to spawn, and those called *anadromous,* which do just the opposite.

The Charles has only one catadromous species, the American eel, which matures in ponds upstream and heads for the Atlantic and its Sargasso Sea to reproduce.

As for anadromous fish, the most numerous that spawn in the Charles are two species of river herring called alewives (*Alosa pseudoharengus*) and blueback herring (*Alosa aestivalis*). It takes a biologist to tell them apart, and people commonly lump both kinds of river herring under the name alewife. In April and May of each year millions of them, typically ten or eleven inches long, crowd into the rivers and brooks of eastern Massachusetts, and the run up the Charles is as strong as any, according to Randall B. Fairbanks of the state's Division of Marine Fisheries. Upstream, each female spawns from 60,000 to 100,000 eggs, which are immediately fertilized with male sperm and sink to the bottom. The adults then return to the sea, and the newborns follow them the next summer or fall. (An "alewife" is a woman who keeps an alehouse, but lexicographers are at sea over whether the fish's name derives from that fact or from some French or Indian word.)

Other anadromous species in the Charles are rainbow smelt and American shad. The smelt make a modest spawning run in the springtime. The story of the shad is the story of the big one that got away — and is now coming back after a long absence.

The American shad (*Alosa sapidissima*), the largest member of the herring family, sometimes called "the poor man's salmon," used to enter the Charles to spawn, but stopped early in this century. The stoppage was probably due to pollution and the Charles River Dam of 1908. In the 1970s the state's fish experts began an effort to bring back the shad. The species was available in the Connecticut River, but shad are too fragile for easy transport; so shad roe were stripped from shad in the Connecticut and broadcast in the Charles. The eggs sank without a trace of offspring.

Wood duck

Chain pickerel

Then the experts devised a circular fish-stocking tank with a whirlpool effect, and in it, beginning in 1978, they hauled more than one thousand pre-spawning shad from the Connecticut River to the middle Charles every spring. Some juveniles were seen as early as 1980 — proof that spawning had taken place. It was hoped that the juveniles were reaching the sea and that they would eventually come back to spawn, but no one knew for sure.

At about 9:30 in the morning of May 24, 1984, Phillips D. Brady, a marine fisheries biologist for the state, arrived at the Watertown Dam, just upstream from Watertown Square. The day before, he had set a wire–mesh trap at the top of the dam's fishway, which is a sort of switchback staircase similar to the one shown in the picture. Brady slid shut a rear gate on his trap and immediately saw that he had captured a shad swimming there. It proved to be a male, nineteen inches long, weighing two and a half pounds, and it was obviously on its journey to the scene of its birth — an event which presumably occurred in 1980. This was exciting fish news, and the specimen has been mounted by a taxidermist.

Three other returning shad were caught that spring, and six were confirmed in 1985. Though the numbers were small, this

Drawn by Susanah Brown for *Harvard Magazine.*

Largemouth bass

Young American shad

"first documentation of ascending adults" indicated, according to Brady, "that efforts by state and local authorities to improve the water quality and condition of the Charles River are being rewarded."

Anyone blocking a waterway used by migratory fish is legally bound to provide passage. The new Charles River Dam contains two fishways costing $500,000. One of these, an innovative arrangement intended to allow passage when the tide is higher than the Basin and the sluices are closed, has not functioned satisfactorily, but the alewives and smelt have had no trouble getting through the three locks. They go through with boats, and

The fishway at the Wellesley end of the Finlay Dam. At left is the Route 16 bridge between Wellesley and Newton. Here the river flows northward, from right to left, and the white water showing at upper center is at the foot of the dam, which is six feet high. A fish going upstream swims up the passage at our left, reverses direction, and emerges on the higher level to the right. The wooden baffles in the passages have V-notched bottom parts (under water) which retard the flow and enable the fish to scoot up by easy stages. (Photograph by Jack Maley, Metropolitan District Commission.)

when the fish show up in large numbers they are locked through even if no boats need passage at the time.

The MDC, moving gradually upstream, is installing fishways at the old dams on the lower half of the Charles. In the summer of 1985 a $92,000 fishway was completed on the Finlay Dam in Lower Falls. The MDC expects to build five more fish passages by the early 1990s. When the final one goes into service on the South Natick Dam, the shad and river herring may spawn all the way up to Medway, sixty miles from the river mouth.

Shad Number One. After years of efforts by the Commonwealth of Massachusetts to revive the shad run in the Charles, this fish, caught in 1984, was the first proof of success. (Photograph by P. D. Brady, Massachusetts Division of Marine Fisheries.)

10   Boats and More Boats

In proportion to its size the Charles must be one of the country's boatingest rivers. Gone are the centuries when sailing vessels brought freight and passengers to Cambridge's Town Creek and beyond. And a different kind of commercial traffic — tugs, barges, tankers, and the like — reached its peak in 1926 and now is near zero. But recreational craft are all over the place, sometimes getting in one another's way. The most outlandish are the rafts that are thrown together once a year for the Charles River Raft Race, an undergraduate event of chaotic merriment sponsored by Harvard's Adams House. As for the serious boat users of the Charles Basin (between Watertown and Charlestown), they come in four main varieties:

• *Sailors.* About 200 sailing boats are based at Community Boating, Inc., and the sailing clubs of M.I.T., Harvard, and Boston University. The sailboats of Community Boating are open to the public at moderate fees and are one of the most conspicuous demonstrations that the Charles belongs to the people. Community Boating is a nonprofit corporation whose officers and directors are volunteers. Its goal is to provide sailing for all — and instruction in sailing — at the lowest cost possible. At a dock and boathouse provided by the MDC, Community Boating since 1950 has carried on a program that was started by others in 1940 and is thought to be the oldest and largest public sailing program in the world. It has been widely imitated. In the 1985 season the institution had 115 sailboats, five safety launches, six rowboats, and ten windsurfers. It had sixty paid employees and a much larger number of volunteer instructors. Community Boating is often said to be the world's largest sailing school. In its junior program alone, around two thousand girls and boys take part, and they are charged one dollar ($1.00) for the entire summer.

• *Scullers and racing crews.* About 350 of their boats frequent the Basin. Boathouses are maintained by three venerable boat clubs — Union, Riverside, and Cambridge — and by four colleges and two prep schools. The Charles is widely known as a center of intensive training for Olympic and other championship competition, and as the site of the annual Head-of-the-Charles Regatta. The oldest of the clubs is the Union Boat Club, which was founded in 1851 on Brimmer Street (then at the brim of the river) and which has maintained its boathouse on Embankment Road ever since the Boston Embankment was created in 1910. This club holds a distinguished place in the history of American rowing. In 1914, eights from the Union Boat Club and Harvard were the first non-English crews to compete at Henley. Both made it to the finals for the Grand Challenge Cup, and Harvard won by about a length.

• *Resident powerboaters.* In 1985, according the the MDC police, 762 powerboats, most of them ocean-going, made their homes at four spots in the Basin, namely the Newton, Watertown, Charlesgate, and Charles River yacht clubs.

• *Transient motorboaters.* These enter the upper Basin at an MDC launching area off Nonantum Road and usually head for the river mouth. About two hundred or more of these trailered craft are apt to enter the Basin on a summer Saturday, and even more on a Sunday. They are the scourge of the rowing community, because some of them go too fast, cause wakes, and reduce fun and safety on the Charles.

Rowers and sailors complain that MDC traffic regulations have been poorly enforced. The Metropolitan Police say that they are acutely conscious of the problem, that their officers in patrol boats give out many citations for illegal behavior, and that many offenders have been fined or even jailed. They point out that it is no more possible to prevent all river speeding than to prevent all highway speeding. Nevertheless, as the number of boats increases year by year, safety on the Charles — indeed the whole question of competing uses of the Basin — is one of the most serious problems that the MDC faces in the eighties and nineties.

On the river above the Basin there are several kinds of small craft, but the ruling favorite is the canoe. Reverently the Charles River Watershed Association says in its booklet *Charles River Canoe Guide:* "The silence of a canoe moving through the water reinforces the oneness of man with nature. It is without equal for the full enjoyment of the sights and sounds of a river environment."

Canoe racing on the Charles is rising in popularity. Each April the Watershed Association conducts a day of races called the Run of the Charles. The first, in 1983, attracted 358 participants. The number increased to 670 the next year and to 1,059 the next. In 1985 the races were at three distances — 46, 29, and 6½ miles. The contestants, operating in pairs, carry their canoes around dams. The fastest-growing event has been a relay race in which the same canoe is used by successive pairs of paddlers.

Propelling a narrow boat in the Basin is very different from canoeing. Enthusiasts of rowing consider it the supreme form of exercise, and many feel that it is an inspiring, almost mystical experience. Harvard professor emeritus Edward S. Mason, who sculled on the Charles for half a century, told me that he had some of his best ideas while on the river. Gail Pierson Cromwell, recently president of the Cambridge Boat Club, who was national women's 500-meter champion three times in the 1970s while she was teaching economics at Harvard and M.I.T., and who has been a major figure in the rise of women's rowing in America, told me sculling is "like hitting a golf ball exactly right and feeling the force applied to the ball." Sculling gives her "that same sweet sensation." It's physically exhausting but at the same time "completely relaxing, away from the trouble of the world."

I will take her word for it. My own sweet sensation was stepping out of the boat alive. I had never sculled before (sculling is a two-oared activity, whether singles, doubles, or quads, as contrasted with fours and eights in which each member pulls one oar). To do a bit of sculling in preparation for writing about the Charles seemed a reasonable idea. Harry Parker, the Harvard crew coach, arranged matters with Buzz Tarlow at Weld Boathouse.

First I had to pass a swimming test, four laps in the Indoor Athletic Building, a hundred yards in all, without treading water or turning on my back. After two laps I began to realize that I had never swum a hundred yards before. But in the interest of the great reading public I had to do it. Next came several coaching sessions in a tank on the dock. There were half a dozen things to remember simultaneously. After much practice I was not bad at it, though one thumb bloodied the other each time I pulled the sculls toward my chest.

Then they put me in a wherry, slightly wider than a racing shell, and told me to cross the river at Anderson Bridge, go downstream and recross at the Weeks Bridge, then row back upstream. I quickly found that I was utterly unable to see where I was going (my head will not swivel even ninety degrees, much less 180) and that the effort to avoid overturning so absorbed my attention that I forgot all the things I had learned in the tank. There is no point in going into detail about tangling with another boat and continually col-

Sculling is the favorite recreation of a lot of people. This boat is going downstream beneath the Weeks Bridge. Visible through the arch is Dunster House, one of Harvard's residential houses. (Photograph by Jim Harrison for *Harvard Magazine*.)

A day at the races. Crews pass Weeks Bridge in the Head-of-the-Charles Regatta of 1983, as seen from the tower of Harvard's Eliot House. (Photograph by Jim Harrison for *Harvard Magazine*.)

liding with the right bank and then the left. The main thing is that no speedboat happened along and I got back. I wish to take this opportunity of apologizing to Buzz Tarlow for not showing up on the morrow for my next lesson.

The Head-of-the-Charles Regatta, now more than twenty years old, takes place each year on the next-to-last Sunday in October.

The Head-of-the-Charles, "America's Fall Rowing Festival," may be the world's largest rowing event. All that the Cambridge Boat Club claims is that it is the largest held in a single day. It brings together about 3,320 athletes — men and women — in about 720 boats, representing more than two hundred rowing clubs, colleges, high schools, and other organizations in the United States, Canada, and a few other countries. They compete in eight championship events and about seventeen other races for classes such as veterans, youths, and lightweights. All the events are in single sculls, double sculls, fours, and eights.

Large crowds assemble to watch the unusual spectacle. The course is three miles long in an upstream direction, beginning downstream of the Boston University Bridge and ending about half a mile above the Eliot Bridge. (Intercollegiate races on the Charles also go in an upstream direction but are only 2,000 meters, with Harvard Bridge at the halfway point.) In the Head-of-the-Charles Regatta, the boats in each race cross the starting line at full speed in single file, about fifteen seconds apart, and continually change their order as superior boats pass slower ones. Each boat is timed by computer.

The Head-of-the-Charles was founded in 1965 by two members of the Cambridge Boat Club, D'Arcy MacMahon and Howard McIntyre. They consulted Ernest Arlett, an Englishman who was then a sculling instructor at Weld Boathouse. He convinced them they ought to have a head-of-the-river race — an ancient custom in England. "Head" simply means the winner, or champion; thus a "head of the Charles" is crowned each year in each event.

So MacMahon and McIntyre introduced the system to this continent and kept on increasing the number of events to attract a wide participation. As the regatta expanded under Cambridge Boat Club sponsorship, many other waterways in the U.S. and Canada acquired their "head" regattas. A few examples are: Head-of-the-Potomac, Head-of-the-Schuylkill, Head-of-the-Rideau, Head-of-the-Connecticut, and Head-of-the-Chattahoochee.

11 The People's River

Though the Charles is the people's river, the pleasures of the metropolitan water park are somewhat marred by the streams of automobiles whizzing along its banks. Much depends on your point of view. If you live in the Back Bay and want to stroll down to the water's edge you may have to stroll pretty far until you find a pedestrian overpass. If you are in your car, and in a hurry, you may be glad of the roadways; and you will also enjoy the vista as you ride, especially if someone else is driving.

In Cambridge a limited counterattack has been made against riverbank traffic hazards. On Sundays during the six months of daylight saving time, Memorial Drive for one and a half miles, from the Western Avenue Bridge to the Eliot Bridge, is closed to traffic so that the residents (including roller skaters and bicyclists) can swarm freely over the pavement. The enlarged recreation area of roadway and grassy beach is called "Riverbend Park." It is the brainchild of Isabella Halsted of Cambridge. She kept after the MDC until it agreed to the weekly closure, and her organization, People for Riverbend Park, shares the operating expenses with the MDC.

But the "people's river" motif is most dramatically illustrated by the free symphony concerts and fireworks in the lower Basin.

Arthur Fiedler (1894–1979) chose the Esplanade for the fulfillment of a dream — free concerts by members of the Boston Symphony, outdoor music for the people, an outlandish idea that was

Fireworks in the lower Basin on July 4, 1985. They were designed and fired by Ken Clark, head of Pyrotechnology, Inc. (Photograph by Dan Walsh.)

Scenes of Riverbend Park, the name given to the Cambridge shore from the Western Avenue Bridge to the Eliot Bridge, on Sundays during the months of daylight saving time, when Memorial Drive is closed to automobiles. (Pictures were taken September 29, 1985, by Nancy Hall.)

resisted and scoffed at. He made it a success, and conducted the Esplanade Concerts for fifty years, beginning in 1929. The first two music shells built on the site had disabilities. Then, under the will of Maria E. Hatch, the Edward Hatch Memorial Shell was built in 1939, a memorial to her brother. And all was well.

The story of the Esplanade Concerts is told by Harry Ellis Dickson in his book *Arthur Fiedler and the Boston Pops.* The most spectacular of the concerts, on July 4, 1976, the bicentennial of U.S. independence, was attended by an estimated 400,000 people. They crowded the Esplanade and Storrow Drive and watched from boats on the river. Millions more heard the program on radio and television. As always on the Fourth of July, the program included Tchaikovsky's Overture 1812, with cannon and church bells. The fireworks launched from barges seemed especially brilliant and loud that night. This event was the highlight of Fiedler's career. And it was a highlight in the history of the Charles.

Up the lazy river in the peaceful countryside there are no events of such crashing splendor. But consider the Adopt-A-Brook program of the Charles River Watershed Association. In Dover, Noanet Brook has been adopted by the Noanett (sic) Garden Club, which not only works to preserve the stream's beauty but has collected water samples that warned of a dangerously low level of alkalinity. In Millis, Troop 15 of the Boy Scouts is the guardian of Eagle Brook. In Bellingham, the Stall Brook Elementary School and one of its teachers, Lori Fafard, are energetic guardians of Stall Brook, which borders the school playground. Indeed, Stall Brook is part of the curriculum, for this school is strong on environmental education. In the mid-eighties, about thirty tributaries have been adopted, and about fifty others are waiting for their foster parents.

Through modest enterprises of that sort, not just through the projects of the federal, state, and local governments, the people of the Charles Valley are celebrating their river.

Index

About the Author

Max Hall is a free-lance writer living in Cambridge, the author of books and articles on Harvard history and many other subjects. His books include *Harvard University Press: A History* and *Benjamin Franklin and Polly Baker, The History of a Literary Deception.* He has been a journalist in Atlanta, New York, and Washington, and was a Nieman Fellow at Harvard in 1949–50. From 1930 to 1973 he was Social Science Editor of Harvard University Press. His article "The People's River" in *Harvard Magazine* won two prizes and was the forerunner of this book.

The Charles

has been set in a film version of Trump Mediæval, a typeface designed by Professor Georg Trump in the mid-1950s and cast by the C. E. Weber Typefoundry of Stuttgart, West Germany. The roman letter forms of Trump Mediæval are based on classical prototypes, but have been interpreted by Professor Trump in a distinctly modern style. The italic letter forms are more of a sloped roman than a true italic in design, a characteristic shared by many contemporary typefaces. The result is a modern and distinguished type, notable both for its legibility and its versatility.

The book was designed by David Ford. The calligraphy was done by Charles C. Hefling Jr. The type was set by the Office of the University Publisher of Harvard University. The paper is Glatco Matte, an entirely acid-free sheet. Holyoke Lithograph Company was the printer and binder.